TI
isle of
# by tram,
train and foot

by
Stan Basnett
and
David Freke

Edited by Stan Abbott

Picture shows the Manx Electric Railway at Ballaglass where it is crossed on Walk 3, page 58. Beyond, rare traces of snow dust the flanks of the Cornaa Valley in a scene typical of the countryside that surrounds the wild heart of the island

Dedication

From The Lanes of Ellan Vannin, a poem of uncertain origin
When Springtime in its beauty wakes up our lovely Isle,
And happy birds are singing, oh isn't life worthwhile,
In the lanes of Ellan Vannin, see nature's own rebirth,
The lambkins in the meadow and the clean sweet tang of earth.

First published 1990 by Leading Edge Press and Publishing Ltd,
The Old Chapel, Burtersett, Hawes, North Yorkshire, DL8 3PB.
☎ (0969) 667566. ISBN 0 948135 14 X.

ISBN, 1992 edition: 0 948135 42 5

British Library Cataloguing in Publication Data

A CIP Catalogue record for this book is available from the British Library.

RailTrail Series editor, and designer: Stan Abbott

Sketch maps by Stan Basnett based on the *Isle of Man Public Rights of Way and Outdoor Leisure Map*, with the permission of the Isle of Man planning department

Type: Leading Edge Press & Publishing Ltd

Colour reprographics: Impression, Leeds

Printed and bound in Great Britain by Ebenezer Baylis and Son Ltd, Worcester

RailTrail series logo by Barbara Drew

The publishers would particularly like to thank the following organisations for their help in producing this book:
The Isle of Man Department of Tourism and Transport
Isle of Man Steam Packet Seaways

Contents

All text by Stan Basnett, with the
exception of the Historical Section,
by David Freke

Publisher's notes

NOTWITHSTANDING the best efforts of the Isle of Man Department of Tourism, people in the UK usually harbour grave misconceptions about this British dependency at the centre of the Irish Sea.

For many, the name conjures up images only of rich tax exiles, or motorcycle races. For others, the picture is of a sort of offshore Blackpool. Relatively few will speak romantically of rolling heather-clad hills — steeped in history — that fall into plunging cliffs which guard secluded coves on some of the most dramatic coastline in the British Isles.

But this, for those who have troubled to visit the island, is the true Manx picture.

It is the combination of history, culture, great natural beauty and a truly remarkable vintage railway system that is the inspiration for this book, and indeed for Leading Edge's entire *RailTrail* series.

The island's steam trains are no strangers to literary inspiration, reputedly being the model for the Rev W Awdry's *Thomas the Tank Engine* books.

And now the remarkable electric railway is in the spotlight as preparations are made for the celebration of its centenary, for which this book is one of the official publications.

I hope you enjoy the train rides and the walks and learn to love the Isle of Man as I do.

Stan Abbott, RailTrail Series Editor, North Yorkshire, June 1992

Note: Manx was predominantly a spoken language and hence there are many variations in the way names are spelt today. The place names appearing in the text of this book are taken from Kneen's *The Place Names of the Isle of Man* and often differ, for example, from those appearing on the Ordnance Survey map.

The sketch maps of walks are intended as a guide only and it is recommended, particularly on the longer walks, that the OS *Landranger*, sheet 95, is carried. Better still, is the 1:25,000 scale *Public Rights of Way* map published by the Isle of Man Government, price £4.

The authors:

STAN BASNETT was born in Douglas in 1938 and educated in the town. He has lived and worked all his life on the Isle of Man and — a chartered surveyor — he was the Isle of Man Government's Surveyor General, before taking up his present post as Assistant Commercial Manager at the Isle of Man Post Office.

He is married with two grown-up daughters. His interests include all aspects of Manx heritage, transport, photography, running, cycling and — above all — walking, with his wife, Carol.

DAVID FREKE was, at the time of writing his contribution to this book, employed by Liverpool University and was in charge, from 1982 to 1990, of the dramatic excavation of remains at Peel Castle and the drawing-up of a report on the important finds made there.

He is a Fellow of the Society of Antiquaries and Member of the Institute of Field Archaeologists. He now lives and works in Oxfordshire.

Foreword

BY ROBERT SMITH

Chief Executive, Isle of Man Transport

WHEN I WROTE the foreword to the first edition of this book, our winter train service was in operation and the staff of Isle of Man Railways were busy catching up on the various maintenance tasks that build up during a busy summer season. It all seemed a far cry from my previous job as a manager with London Transport which I left four years ago to fulfil every schoolboy's dream and take charge of a complete railway system!

Of course, the Isle of Man's railways are quite unique — in the Isle of Man Steam Railway, the Manx Electric and the Snaefell Mountain Railway we can point proudly to working examples of Victorian and Edwardian engineering. The sheer scale of its operations makes Isle of Man Railways the largest vintage railway operator in the British Isles.

In all, we have more than 37 miles of track, 22 miles of it — the Manx Electric and Snaefell lines — double. In spring, additional seasonal staff join our ranks to help us carry around 170,000 people a year.

At a time when the Manx tourist industry must stand or fall on how well we promote the island's rich heritage, our remarkable historic railways are an invaluable asset — a fact which our Government is proud to recognise. We at Isle of Man Railways are pleased to be able to justify that confidence by taking an increasing share of the visitor market on a not-to-be forgotten ride.

The forthcoming celebrations of the Manx Electric Railway Centenary in 1993 will provide us with the opportunity to show off our railways to the widest possible audience. A series of special events throughout the year will ensure our reputation is carried ever further.

Recent times have been exciting ones for us as we carry out important improvements to rolling stock, depots and stations throughout the system. It's surprising what can be achieved with the support of dedicated staff who show so much enthusiasm and inventiveness. We have already won a Railway Heritage Award for work on Laxey station, and Port Erin station reopened in 1990 after careful renovation.

We are keen to support any initiative that will encourage more people to discover the remarkable heritage of our railways and the stunning coastline and countryside they pass through. This book from Leading Edge's *RailTrail* series has become a minor classic since the publication of the first edition and I am happy to endorse this updated version as one of the publications permitted to carry our 1993 MER Centenary emblem.

I hope that, having come and ridden on our trains and seen our sights, you will encourage your friends to come and share the Manx experience.

RS, Douglas, June 1992

Photographic credits

SB — *Stan Basnett*
SA — *Stan Abbott*
PF — *PictureFolio*
DT — *Isle of Man Department of Tourism*

Page 1 — MER at Ballaglass, SB
p7 — Cashtal yn Ard, SB
p8 — Meayl Hill, SA
p 11 — Tynwald, TB
p15 — Field patterns, Dalby, SA
p19 — Foxdale mines, Basnett collection
p23 — IMR at Ballacarry, SB
p26 — IMR at Gob y Deigan, SB; IMR crest, SA
p30 — MER, Laxey, SA
p17 — Peel, PF
p20 — North Bradda, SB
p21 — Snaefell Mines, SB
p24 — IMR, Santon, SB
p25 — MER at Ballure, SB
p29 — Douglas harbour, PF
p31 — SMR, Bungalow, SB
p35 — Douglas promenade, SB
p37 — Victoria Street, SR Keig
p38 — Cable tram, SR Keig
p39 — Tower of Refuge, SB
p40 — Douglas horse tram, SA
p41 & 42 — Peel Castle, SA
p43 — Herring smoking, DT; Viking, SA
p44 — Peel station, SB; Peel, SA
p47 — Castletown, SA
p50 — Ramsey, DT
p52 — Groudle Glen Railway, SA
p53 — Groudle old zoo; Laxey, both SA; horse trams, SB
p56 — Laxey Wheel, three pix, SA
p58 — Cashtal yn Ard, SB
p62 & 63 — Marine Drive, SB
p65 — Rushen Abbey, SB
p67 — Monks' Bridge & Rushen Abbey, both DT
p68 — Derby Fort, SB
p70 — Cregneash, DT
p71 — Cregneash, SA
p72 — Cornelly mines, SB

p74 — Foxdale mines, Basnett collection
p75 — Foxdale station, Basnett collection
p76 — Tynwald, SA
p83 — Laxey Station, SB
p85 — Laxey mines C1920, WC Souhtward
p87 — Above Snaefell mines, SB
p94 — Peel harbour, DT
p97 — Lag ny Killey hermitage, SA
p99 — Cronk ny Irrey Laa summit, SB
p100 — Bradda Head,SB
p103 — Calf of Man, SB
p104 — Chasms, SB
p105 — Sugar Loaf and Scarlett rocks, SB
p108 — Douglas Bay, SB
p114 — Niarbyl and Dalby, SA
p117 — Mine at Dhoon Glen, SB
p123 — IMR, Union Mills; IMR, St John's, SB
p125 — Dhoon Glen, SB
p126 — Manx cat, DT; Loaghtan sheep, SA

History of the Isle of Man

Stones of history — Cashtal yn Ard

THE Manx people owe their history and destiny to the island's position at the centre of the north Irish Sea. In days when the movement of people and goods by sea was far easier than by land, the Isle of Man stood at the veritable "crossroads" of what has been called the "British Mediterranean". The island lies within sight of Ulster, 45 miles (70 km) away, Galloway (22 miles), Cumbria (30 miles), and the North Wales coast, 62 miles to the south.

This apparent intimacy, and the usefulness to mariners of the mountain peaks on the Isle of Man and the two mainlands as aids to navigation, were offset only by the dangers of the at times wild and unpredictable sea.

Once, the Isle of Man was linked to mainland Britain, but it became an island as sea levels rose after the last Ice Age (about 7000BC). This meant that some of the large mammals and slower reptiles never reached the island, which developed its own varieties of other species. Today, although the island's mild climate is friendly to a variety of introduced plants, its early isolation has led to less variety in the native flora and fauna, compared with Ireland and Britain.

Despite the mountainous heart of the island, there are large areas of good agricultural land, mainly on the northern plain and in the south and east, and so the island has, through history, been an attractive possession prized for its potential wealth, as evidenced in the *Chronicles of the Kings of Mann and the Isles*. A dispute arose in the 13th century when Reginald, King of Mann, gave his brother Olaf the larger, but much poorer, island of Lewis, thereby provoking a conflict which led to the death of Reginald, the mutilation of Olaf, civil war and desolation on Man, until the intervention of the King of Norway.

The island's economic and strategic attractiveness has meant that it has rarely been left to its own devices for very long. In the last 1,500 years, Welsh, Irish, Scottish, English and Scandinavian interests have at various times felt obliged to control the Isle of Man in pursuit of their own wider territorial or military ambitions, thereby shaping its present day landscape and institutions.

These episodes of domination have often been marked by military struggles, both on the island or involving islanders elsewhere, which have seriously impoverished the small community. The periods of calm between these storms saw the building of Isle of Man's distinctive cultural identity.

Pre-history

The present "natural" environment is the product of the exploitation of the land by people since the earliest period of human occupation of the island. The peat in Lough Cranstal, north of Bride, has been found to contain charcoal dated to 5500 BC, suggesting that the early hunters and gatherers who settled on the island were burning the forest to concentrate game in artificial clearings.

Archaeologists have found evidence — including flint spear tips and hazel nuts — that these Mesolithic people lived on the island between about 8000 and 4000 BC.

The burial monuments are the most enduring mark left on the Manx landscape by the first Neolithic (4000 to 1800 BC) farmers. There seem to have been two early groups. One has been called the *Cashtal yn Ard* group, after the dramatic megalithic tomb of that name near Maughold — *see Walk 3, page 57.*

This is a large stone structure with a forecourt and chambers at the west end, and a heap of fire-reddened stones at the east, all originally covered by a cairn. The large upright stones around the forecourt and the kerbstones of the two phases of the cairn can still be seen, although some of them have been re-erected.

The similar, very damaged, although originally much larger, tomb called King Orry's Grave can be seen on the hill above Laxey, near the Minorca tram halt.

These tombs were communal burial places, where the bones of a whole community were laid to rest. It is probable that each settlement had a tomb, visible from the settlement or the scattered farms, but no dwellings from this time have been found yet on the island.

The other early farmers —

the *MeaylHill* group — lived at the same time as the Cashtal yn Ard people, and sometimes pottery made by both peoples is found together on archaeological sites. The tombs of the Meayll group are best represented by the fine passage grave on Meayl Hill itself, near Cregneash— *see Walk 8, page 70.*

It comprises six pairs of stone chambers, each pair entered through a short passage at right angles to it, and thus forming a T-shape. The pairs are arranged in a circle. The whole was originally covered by a cairn, with possibly a primary "cist" burial, or stone-lined grave, in the centre. This monument is unique, and must be an insular version of the widely distributed passage grave.

Bronze Age

The Bronze Age (about 1800 to 800 BC) seems to fall into "early" and "late" periods, marked by dramatic changes in burial ritual, artefacts, social organisation and climate.

In the early Bronze Age, the funerary rite changed from the Neolithic communal cemeteries to cairns and earth mounds — barrows — covering central burials. Secondary interments then often took place, sometimes with an enlargement of the mound. The primary burials were sometimes placed in stone cists like the one at St John's in the roadside bank, adjacent to Tynwald Hill, itself a probable early burial mound — *see Walk 9, page 72.*

Part of the circular burial site at Meayl Hill

There are many mounds on the island which may be Bronze Age barrows, often in prominent locations such as Cronk ny Irrey Laa — see *Manx Meander, Stage 6, page 97*.

Like their Neolithic counterparts, they were probably visible from the settlements and fine upland examples may be seen on either side of the main road south west of Dalby Mountain. There are others in the lowlands, like those around Bride and Andreas.

The late Bronze Age seems to be a time of increasing pressure on resources, perhaps made more acute by another climatic deterioration which made upland farming untenable. In Britain, hill forts begin to appear at about this time which is interpreted as evidence of increasing tension. In Man, the major hillfort on South Barrule was functioning in the late Bronze Age.

Iron Age

Devotees of the TV series, *Lovejoy*, may recall an episode in which a group of rogues in the antique trade perpetrated a scam based on the idea that Roman remains had, for the first time, been found on the Isle of Man. In fact, the Romans never invaded the island and so the Manx Iron Age ran from about 500 BC to AD 600.

But whatever the Romans' activities, Manx society in those days clearly felt threatened by enemies both within and without, as known Iron Age sites on the island are mostly well defended or in inaccessible locations.

This period saw the construction of coastal promontary forts, presumably to guard against seaborne attack, at Close ny Chollagh (*see Manx Meander, Stage 7, p104*), Cronk ny Merriu (*Meander, Stage 8, p107*), Cass ny Hawin (*Meander, Stage 8*), *p107*, Langness Point, near Derbyhaven, and as many as 18 more around the Manx coast.

As well as inland fortified homesteads at Ballanicholas, just south of the Millenium Way between Crosby and St Mark's, and Castleward, near Strang on the outskirts of Douglas (*Manx Meander, Stage One, page 83*) there are the defended hilltop sites at Cronk Sumark (*Manx Meander, Stage Three,*), Maughold Head (*Walk 4, page 59*), Burroo Ned and Chapel Hill (*both passed on Stage 7 of the Manx Meander*), and the later defences of South Barrule. So the Iron Age presents a picture of both communal and individual defence.

The recent excavations at St Patrick's Isle, Peel, have unearthed a pre-Christian village where access was inconvenient enough for it to have been chosen for security reasons. A large grain store was discovered, which suggests a centralised accumulation of staple goods for financial and political control. The village on the islet may have been a chieftain's stronghold.

Three large low round mounds near Castletown were excavated in the 1940s. They were up to 30 yards in diameter and proved to have been round houses with up to six concentric circles of supporting posts.

Late Iron Age and early Christianity

The Roman invasion of England made the Irish Sea an important frontier zone and the Emperor Agricola considered invading Ireland in AD 81-82. He carried out intelligence gathering operations but chose instead to take his fleet and armies to south-west Scotland, leaving Ireland and Man undisturbed.

The Roman fleet which policed the shores of Scotland extended the *pax Romana* to the Irish Sea, and emphasised the links between Celtic nations. Mythological heroes — such as Manannan, a personification of the sea, Conchobar, a King of Ulster, Culainn, a Manx smith, and the war chief Finn — give a glimpse of a unified Celtic cultural region.

The Christianity of the Celtic west

had developed through missionary contact from the eastern Mediterranean Coptic Church. They brought an austere Christianity based on isolation and meditation, in contrast with the community-based Roman church.

The collapse of Roman Britain in the early fifth century stimulated the sea routes to the Celtic west, encouraging contact with southern Gaul and the hermitic tradition of Christianity there. Despite the efforts of both St Ninian at Candida Casa (Whithorn, in Galloway) and St Patrick in Ireland, who operated in the region as agents of the Roman Church, it took several centuries for the western Celtic church and the Roman church to come into line.

The northern Irish, and, by implication the Manx, retained the increasingly isolated Celtic forms until 716.

The Isle of Man has an unsurpassed collection of early carved stone crosses. The most spectacular group can be seen at Maughold (see Walk 4, page 59), which seems to have been the principal pre-Norse religious community on Man. The churchyard at Maughold is believed to mark the extent of the monastic precinct.

The island also has more than 200 tiny keeil (chapel) sites, many of which are likely to have been built on the sites of pre-Norse chapels. Several have early Christian crosses built into their walls and almost all are dedicated to early Celtic saints. Most of the keeils served the local community, and are located on farm land.

Some had precinct walls and a tiny circular cell for the hermit. The locations of some of these "hermitages" have clearly been chosen for their spectacular scenery, like Lag ny Killey, half way down a precipitous slope into the sea between Peel and Port Erin, see Manx Meander, Stage Six, and Spooyt Vane, above a dramatic waterfall near Kirk Michael.

The people inhabited round houses not much different from those of their pre-Christian forebears.

The only known village site of this period is at Ronaldsway, now under the airport, where excavations in the late 1930s revealed graves and six round huts. The concentration of prehistoric, early Christian, Viking and medieval occupation around Ronaldsway clearly demonstrates the importance of the area, presumably because of the proximity of a sheltered anchorage and a rich hinterland.

Farmers in those days made use of the marginal land between 500 and 1,000ft for summer pasture. The place name element, Eary, means "summer pasture" and can still be found at the margin of farmland but within the enclosed land. This group of settlements seems to be distinct from the highest settlements, the sheilings, which occur typically above 900ft, on unenclosed open moorland, and which may date from Norse times. See Millenium Way for a good example of these.

The Norse raids and settlement

At the end of the eighth century, Norse adventurers reached the Irish Sea, and Irish annals in 794 record the devastation of "all the islands of Britain". The initial years of Scandinavian presence in the Irish Sea were essentially "Viking", a job description for pirates or raiders. The raids were carried out to gain wealth, and attacks on rich monasteries and churches should be seen as being "pro-loot", rather than "anti-Christian", in motivation.

We can assume that the monastery at Maughold was ransacked and the coastal communities of the Isle of Man harassed in the same way as their counterparts in Ireland. The Vikings must have appreciated the strategic location of the Isle of Man astride the sea routes which were so important for communications in the region.

But the popular picture of "rape and pillage" by marauding Vikings may be giving the settlers — who arrived early in the ninth century — an "unfair press", as it seems the favoured approach was to marry a local woman. Later mixed marriages can be inferred from Norse and Gaelic names on cross slabs, but the most advantageous period for such a strategy would be during the initial settlement, when marriage to local heiresses would greatly facilitate the acquisition of land and wealth.

The Norse incomers were pagans and the Isle of

The "modern" Tynwald mid-summer's parliament has its origins in the Norse "Thing"

Man has an impressive series of more than 20 burial mounds believed to be those of the first settlers.

Three characteristic boat burials have been identified, and the excavation of two other mounds has revealed coffin burials. The rich array of goods discovered in these graves includes swords, spears, axes and shields as well as horse harnesses and, in one case, blacksmith's tools. Many of these finds can be seen in the Manx Museum at Douglas.

An elaborate burial ritual is hinted at by a human sacrifice at Ballateare, and the probability of it at Balladoole.

Pieces of Scandinavian gear have been recovered from a number of early Chris-

tian cemeteries and the recent Peel Castle excavations have revealed a burial ground in use from pre-Norse to late medieval times, apparently without a break. One of the Norse graves is the richest accompanied woman's burial of the period yet discovered outside the Scandinavian homelands. Among the domestic items buried with the woman was a necklace of more than 70 glass, amber and jet beads, indicating her status in the community.

Raiding parties would spend winter on the Isle of Man before sallying forth on summer campaigns. Some of the small Iron Age promontary forts referred to previously contain Norse-style long houses, and the watch site at Vowlan, on the sea front north of Ramsey, was occupied in Norse times — *see Ramsey Town Trail, page 48.*

The control of the sea also lies behind the fortification of St Patrick's Isle. Recent excavations inside the medieval castle have revealed a stone rampart on the eastern edge of the islet, the only side not naturally protected by cliffs. It has been dated to the 11th or 12th century, and may be one of the forts King Magnus Barefoot built in 1098.

This was the Isle of Man's principal Norse stronghold, defending the sheltered harbour and the central valley.

Later Norse kings of Man lived on St Patrick's Isle—Magnus Barefoot landed at St Patrick's Isle in 1098, and the Norse kings Godred II and Olaf II died there in 1187 and 1237 respectively. The Iron Age hill fort at Cronk Sumark, referred to previously, may have been refortified as there is a striking similarity between its layout and that of Dark Age sites in Scotland and Wales.

From the vantage point of Cronk Sumark it would have been possible for the Norse settlers to watch over and co-ordinate the defence of the fertile northern plain and its sea approaches.

The pagan Norse had, by the late tenth century, been converted to Christianity, leading to a veritable flowering of Norse carving, some of which shows an appreciation of both Christian and pagan motifs. Thorwald's cross at Andreas depicts Odin and Fenris at Ragnarok on one side, while, on the other, is a figure holding aloft a book and a cross while trampling a serpent.

The Norse kingdom of Mann and the Isles

The history of the Isle of Man becomes more focussed with the coming of Godred Crovan, the King Orry of Manx legend. He was a survivor of Harald Hadrada's army— defeated at Stamford Bridge, Yorkshire, in 1066 — who took refuge on the Isle of Man. In 1079, at the battle of Sky Hill, near Ramsey *(visited on Stage 3 of the Manx Meander and the Millenium Way)* he defeated the Manx at the third attempt and welded together an extensive island kingdom which encompassed the western Scottish isles.

After his death, on Islay in 1095, there was a period of civil war which was to the advantage of Magnus Barefoot, King of Norway. He subsequently used the Isle of Man as a base from which to harass the coasts of Wales and Ireland, before he eventually came to grief in an ill-starred attempt to invade Ireland in 1103.

The descendents of Godred Crovan then ruled the Isle of Man until the death of Magnus II, the last Norse King of Man, in 1265. In the reign of Godred II (1153-87) the Manx kings lost control of the islands of Mull and Islay, retaining only the Lewis and Skye groups, and the Isle of Man found itself increasingly caught between warring factions representing Scottish, English and Norwegian interests.

Scandinavian administrative and cultural customs became established with the settlement. The Manx parliament, Tynwald, has evolved from the *Thing*, the Norse procedure for settling disputes. The 24 members of the Manx House of Keys are elected, their number reflecting the other islands in the original Kingdom of Man.

The ten-strong Legislative Council is elected by the Keys. Tynwald now sits in Douglas but on the old midsummer day, July 5, an open-air sitting is held at St John's on the tiered earthen mound of Tynwald Hill. Here, amid considerable pomp, the legislation enacted by Tynwald during the previous year is announced to the assembled populace in English and Manx. St John's Church is symbolically linked to the Hill by a ceremonial procession whose way is strewn with rushes, originally a tribute to Manannan the Celtic sea god.

The climatic improvement in the 11th and 12th centuries encouraged the exploitation of higher land. Livestock would be driven to upland pastures — shielings — in the summer, and the people lived in small turf-walled huts where evidence of cheese-making and weaving has been found.

The Viking incursions seem to have delayed the Church's adoption of the full Roman parochial system. The monastery of St Maughold retained its pre-eminent position, probably until St German's Cathedral on St Patrick's Isle was established in the late 12th or early 13th century.

In 1134, King Olaf I (1113-53) invited the monks of Furness to found an Abbey at Ballasalla, where substantial ruins of their Cistercian house can still be seen — *see Walk.6, page 65*. Rushen Abbey became a focus for the consolidation of the Roman church, with responsibilty for spreading Roman rites and administration.

The siting of the cathedral on St Patrick's Isle emphasised the sacred character of the islet, which already had three churches and a Celtic-style round tower, and which had been used since pre-Norse times as a burial ground. Bishop Simon (1227-1247) is credited with building St German's Cathedral, although the present structure is obviously the accumulated result of several building episodes.

The ceding of the Isle of Man to the Scots, by Norway in 1266, led to almost a century of dispute between Scotland and England, of which the Manx bore the brunt. Manx claims foundered at the battle of Ronaldsway in 1275 when their army was defeated by the Scots. Edward I of England took possession at the end of the 13th century and the island became a royal gift, first to Bailliol, then to the Bishop of Durham, then to Piers Gaveston, the favourite of Edward II.

Robert Bruce intervened to restate Scottish claims in 1313, when his army landed at Ramsey and proceeded south to the capital at Castletown to besiege Castle Rushen, which surrendered after a month. The castle was reputedly virtually destroyed, and Bruce granted the Isle of Man to the Earl of Moray.

The lack of strong government left the island open to an attack by Irish freebooters in 1316, and Scots and English claims were pursued through attacks on each other's forces on the Island in 1329 and 1388. More trouble can be inferred from truces agreed in 1318, 1328, 1333, and "protection money" paid to the Scots in 1343. The island's distress was no doubt an encouragement to the French who, in 1377, also extorted money from the Manx to prevent them burning houses.

During this period, a succession of Scots and English Lords were granted the island by their respective monarchs. Sir William de Montecute was granted the island in absolute possession in 1333, and it was inherited by his his son, the second Earl of Salisbury, in 1344. In 1392, excercising his absolute right of ownership, he sold the island and its crown to a supporter of Richard II, Sir William le Scrope, who — on the accession of Henry IV, in 1399 — was beheaded, leaving the island in the hands of the English Crown again.

Henry granted the island to Henry de Percy, Earl of Northumberland, but after the Percys' rebellion in 1403 it was seized by the Crown. In 1405, it was again handed over to Sir John Stanley — on the service of rendering, as a token of homage, two falcons to Henry, and to all future monarchs of England at their coronation.

During the several centuries of almost unbroken Stanley rule that followed, the island enjoyed relative stability. Nonetheless, the life of the islanders was undoubtedly very hard. The attacks of outsiders were compounded by the rise of the power of the church, which — although it too suffered from attack, steadily increased taxes and the range of activities liable to tithes.

In 1291, tithes were introduced on fish, and the products of merchants, smiths and other craftsmen. In 1302, a punitive "smoke tax" on hearths was imposed and visitation dues were introduced in 1334. Within the church itself there was a struggle for control being fought between the monasteries and the pope. The Pope slowly established his ascendancy and, from 1348, the bishops were obliged to go to him for their consecration. Before this date the Bishop of Sodor and Man was consecrated by the Archbishop of Trondhjem in Norway.

The bishop amassed a considerable proportion of the land, comprising 99 farms and 77 cottages, and he held his own courts, maintaining his own prison in Peel Castle. Other lands in the island were held by Furness Abbey, through Rushen Abbey, and by abbeys and priories in Bangor, Sabhal, St Bees and Whithorn.

Farm productivity improved as the Cistercian monks of Rushen Abbey sought to ensure their tenants emulated their own efficiency. A number of factors worked against a thriving agriculture, however, including political unrest, exploitation by landlords, worsening climatic conditions in the late middle ages, and the system of land holding, under which the people enjoyed no right of tenure.

Medieval farming was frequently disrupted by warfare and raiding, but some features of the Manx landscape became well established, including the mountain hedge which divided the open moorland pasture from the fields.

In the 13th century, the centre of power moved from Peel Castle to Castle Rushen, reflecting a change in the island's defensive posture. Peel was essentially a defence against seaborne attack but could be easily isolated, relying upon a friendly surrounding populace.

As feudal overlords wrestled for control of the Isle of Man a more compact stronghold was required to defend them and their garrisons against an uncertain hinterland. Although Castletown did not have the advantage of such a good natural harbour as Peel, it did command some of the best farm land on the island and there was reasonable access to the shelter of Derbyhaven.

The castle appears to have been commenced in the 12th century, and, by the end of the Norse period, it had become the headquarters of the Norse kings and Magnus II, the last of their number, died there.

The Earls of Derby and the Dukes of Atholl

The gift of the Island to Sir John Stanley in 1405 led to more than 300 years, with brief interruptions, of Stanley rule — as Kings of Man until 1504, and then as Lords of Man until their line failed in 1736.

Sir John, the first Stanley ruler (1405-1414), did not visit the Isle of Man, but his son, Sir John II (1414-1432), took a great interest in its affairs, and began to reform its administration. In the next 100 years, the visits by the Stanleys were rare and governors effectively ruled on their behalf.

Not until 1627 and the accession of James, the seventh Earl, known as "the Great Stanley", did a Stanley actually reside on the island. He also took the unprecedented step of appointing a Manxman, Edward Christian, as deputy governor — an appointment which was used by Christian ultimately to advance Manx interests in grievances about tithes and land tenure.

At the outbreak of the English Civil War, in 1649, Edward Christian was instructed to raise a militia, an army which he then incited to rebellion. Lord Derby, the seventh Earl, returned and astutely outmanoeuvred Christian at a public meeting he called at Peel Castle, leading to the arrest and imprisonment of Christian.

Although the Earl placated the people with some reforms, he exacerbated a dispute which was to dog Manx affairs for another half century by enforcing a system of leasehold to replace the farmers' rights of tenure in a move designed to re-establish the Lord's original rights over his tenants.

Faced with insecurity of tenure, many Manx people turned to smuggling in the late 17th century. The land tenure problem was resolved by the Act of Settlement in 1704, although the related disputes were not settled until 1866.

The seventh Earl rallied to the Royalist cause in 1651, but the small force he took to Lancashire was overwhelmed at Wigan, the Earl escaping, only to be defeated at Worcester, tried in Chester and executed at Bolton.

The original field boundaries — these are at Dalby — can still be made out where the abandonment of farmsteads has led to the loss of pasture to bracken — see over

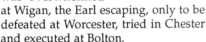

Meanwhile, on the Isle of Man, William Christian — *Illiam Dhone* — rebelled with the militia he had been entrusted to use against the Parliamentarians. He took all the castles except for Peel and Rushen, and offered to surrender the island to Colonel Duckenfield, the leader of the Parliamentary forces.

On hearing the news of her husband's brutal death, the doughty Countess Charlotte eventually surrendered Castle Rushen. The rebels got no better treatment from their new rulers, and ten years later — after the restoration of the monarchy and the Derbys — William Christian was executed at Hango Hill, Castletown, in an act of ill-concealed revenge by Charles Stanley, the eighth Earl.

The religious changes in England in 1540 eventually led to the dissolution of Rushen Abbey and the Nunnery just outside Douglas *(Walks 5 and 6)*, as well as the Friars at Ballabeg in Arbory. The ruined Rushen Abbey at Ballabeg is the last resting place of several Manx kings, and is a picturesque spot near the oldest bridge in the island, only wide enough for a pack horse. The Nunnery is now a much modified private house, and the Friary is part of a farm, its arches incongrously embedded in the farm buildings.

The tenth Earl of Derby (1702-1736) died intestate and the island passed to the second Duke of Atholl, whose family ruled as Lords from 1736 to 1765, and as governors from 1793 until 1830. The British, to halt the smuggling, persuaded the third Duke of Atholl (1764-1765) to part with the island for £70,000. The fourth Duke succeeded in 1774 and agitated for an increase in the sum paid.

He was temporarily mollified by being made Governor-general in 1793, and he built Castle Mona, on the sea front at Douglas, as his residence. His initial popularity was eroded by his habit of nepotism and when, in 1825, his nephew Bishop Murray levied an outrageous potato and turnip tithe there were riots.

The Duke was eventually paid £417,000 by the British Government for his rights, in 1828. This curbed the lucrative smuggling trade, but gave the revenues from Isle of Man taxes to the British with no effective representation for the Manx interest, leading to a period of neglect of capital projects.

Modern times

Until very recently, the Manx were mainly farmers and seafarers — the first island census, in 1726, accounted for 14,426 inhabitants, of whom only 2,530 lived in towns. Douglas had been the largest town since the late 17th century, causing the people of Castletown and Peel to complain that they were unfairly neglected by merchants.

The ninth Earl was very keen to encourage trade, but he recognised that this required a thriving internal economy. In a memorandum of 1698, he set out a programme of improvement which indicated some of the deficiencies of the island, alongside its potential, including its mineral wealth, the exploitation of which is described in the next section.

With the arrival of the later Stanleys, land management became more organised.

The early 19th century, however, saw economic collapse as troops left in 1815, and an act which prevented the recovery of debts contracted oustide the island was repealed. The farming community was exhorted to improve its performance, but many farmers were also fishermen and an account of 1811 notes that four fifths of farming work was carried out by women.

In recent times, the Isle of Man's relationship with its neighbours across the Irish Sea has continued to shape its society and landscape. The late 19th and early 20th century explosion of tourism contributed the elegant sweep of guest houses and hotels round Douglas Bay, and there were similar developments in Port Erin, Port St Mary and Ramsey, while the island also became home to probably the first holiday camp in the British Isles.

The shrinking post-war tourist numbers, paralleled by the rise of the Spanish resorts, has led to the steady erosion of these features, Ramsey being the first to succumb to redevelopment, while the sea front at Douglas now faces a rising demand for office space as hotel accommodation becomes surplus.

Small farms, deserted in the emigrations of the 1820s and 1830s and more recently—leaving overgrown fields and ruined cottages (tholtans) — are being acquired by new residents and, in 1990, the population of the island was rising, partly in response to the increasing saturation of the Channel Islands as "offshore" tax havens.

The island has benefited from the revolution in electronic communications to consolidate the position of financial services as the most important sector of the Manx economy, owing its growth to the attractive financial régime and environmental conditions on the island.

History retains a bold presence on the island, and much of the rich past is well preserved and displayed. Many monuments in the countryside are under the protection of the Manx Museum, with its splendid headquarters in Douglas and specialist outstations in Ramsey (the Grove Museum of Rural Life), Castletown (the castle, the Maritime Museum and the Old Grammar School), the Laxey Wheel, and the working folk life museum run jointly with the Manx National Trust at Cregneash, all of which are included in walks and excursions in this book.

An historical review such as this prompts the question as to how many of the monuments to commerce now rising in Douglas and elsewhere — where older buildings of architectural merit can sometimes enjoy little protection — will remain to be seen by future generations. Will they be regarded with the same respect afforded to the megaliths and mines, keeils and castles, and the trains and trams built in ages when mammon was not god? ❏

This aerial view of Peel from the south shows clearly the strategic value of Peel Island, and — at the same time — its vulnerability should a hostile "mainland" populace seek to isolate it

Industrial heritage

THE industrial heritage of the Isle of Man is dominated by mining and quarrying, in particular mining for metal ores. While the industry is not as old as the Manx hills themselves, there is evidence that lead was mined as long ago as the 13th century, when it was used for roofing the Welsh castles of Edward I.

After the Restoration, in 1660, the search for minerals became more systematic, although the much sought after coal measures were not to be found. But what the Isle of Man may have lacked in this respect, it more than made up for in the wealth of its metal ores.

Indeed, the mineral wealth of the island in the 19th century was outstanding in relation to its size. Today, the marks made by mining on the Manx landscape are extensive.

The industry was also responsible for the creation of settlements which survive today and for other developments, such as the railway line to Foxdale.

In all, a total of 233,292 tons of lead ore, 215,397 tons of zinc ore and 150 tons of silver were recorded as having been produced between 1845 and 1900. Small amounts of copper and iron were also recorded. At the height of the mining boom — in the middle of last century — £80 shares in the Laxey Mining Company were selling at more than £1,000. And small wonder — by 1876, the annual value of ore shipped from Laxey (lead, silver and copper) reached more than £90,000, which was very big money in those days. At Foxdale (lead and silver), the figure consistently approached half this sum.

But, in common with the picture elsewhere in the British Isles, competition saw the decline of the Manx industry, and by 1900 most mines had closed, although Foxdale continued until 1911 and Laxey to 1929.

Early beginnings

The earliest records of mining on the Isle of Man seem to point to Bradda, near Port Erin, in the south of the island where the Great Lode (ore-bearing seam) was exposed for all to see. But what we see now is a huge scar above the remains of the buildings at the South Bradda Mine. Workings probably existed at Port Erin from 1246. Early in the 19th century, the mines were intermittently worked, but by the middle of the century the Bradda Mining Company was operating both the South Bradda and North Bradda mines, producing 364 tons of lead ore and 193 tons of copper ore between 1869 and 1874.

Both mines still show the remains of old galleries and the newer workings, as well as the surface remains of office buildings and engine houses for the pumps. North Bradda mine was sunk to a depth of 72 fathoms (432ft) from the adit (horizontal shaft) a little above sea level. The large surface remains housed the pumping engine, used to lift 200 gallons of sea water per minute from the workings. The working conditions must have been terrible.

The Foxdale Lode was eventually worked underground over a distance of four miles and, although records exist of mining near the surface in the latter part of the 18th century, by the middle of the 19th century, depths of almost 200 fathoms had been reached.

The most westerly mine was Beckwith's, near Glenmaye, where a number of surface remains survive including a rather drunken chimney stack. This mine produced 50,000 tons of lead ore whose value at the time approached £750,000. The mine reached a depth of 185 fathoms, but by 1880 appears to have worked itself out. Almost the last work done was to connect the main adit to Cross's Mine, which stands as a landmark on the saddle between South Barrule and Slieau Whallian and is known as "Snuff

the Wind". Looking east about a quarter of a mile from Cross's Mine are the remains of the surface buildings and the two shafts of Dixon's Mine. By 1868 it had ceased working.

At Foxdale itself there was by far the greatest activity, with a number of shafts being sunk at several locations and eventually all coming under the control of the Isle of Man Mining Company in 1828. Mining started in the early part of the 18th century with surface working of the exposed Foxdale vein which continued in a west-east direction.

The three main shafts at Foxdale, of which some surface remains exist, start with the most westerly, Bawden's Shaft. This was sunk to a depth of 260 fathoms by 1902, after it was opened in 1855. Beckwith's shaft had reached 320 fathoms by the same date and was said to be hot in its lower levels. The third shaft was Potts which bottomed at 200 fathoms. There was a distance of 750 yards between the two extreme shafts, although the length of the underground workings was 1,510 yards, with galleries and levels almost every ten fathoms.

Nowadays, it is hard to imagine the original extent of these workings and the many buildings on the surface, the numerous water wheels, steam engines and other paraphernalia. How were they transported to these comparatively remote areas at that time? Some of the answers are to be found in the Manx National Museum where documents and photographs exist to illustrate how the gargantuan challenge was met.

More than 300 men worked at Laxey, and 350 at Foxdale, and in the third quarter of last century, about 1,000 people were working in the industry throughout the island. Photographs show that women and children were also employed. Where did they all live? If you go to Foxdale, sit up on the Shoulder Road near the entrance to South Barrule slate quarry and look over

Foxdale mines in their heyday last century

Foxdale, pick out some of the features and let your mind drift back in time — see *Walk 9*.

While you do that, just consider also that, from these mines in the latter half of the 19th century, a total of 149,063 tons of lead ore was extracted by hand, from which about 50 tons of silver was also won. The mines in the area were driven through slate at the upper levels, and ended in granite.

The Laxey vein ran in a north-south direction and although not as productive as Foxdale in respect of lead ore it had a high output of zinc blende. The lead, however, produced silver of exceptional quality.

The earliest records of mining at Laxey date from 1781 with adits being driven from Glen Mooar following surface exposures. By 1822 the Lonan Mining Company had been established and, under the direction of the mine's captain, Richard Rowe, extensive works were commenced to develop the area and extend the two shafts which were at this time 130 fathoms deep. Washing floors were built lower down the valley and the crowning glory was the building of a wheel to pump the water from the mine. This was completed in 1847,

but it was not the wheel that can be seen today. It was, however, designed by the same man, Robert Casement, the mine's engineer, and it was at that time the largest wheel in the island.

In 1848 the Laxey Mining Company was formed and employed almost as many men as the Foxdale mines. By 1854 the company name was changed yet again to the Great Laxey Mining Company and, the same year, the Great Laxey Wheel was commissioned with much pomp and circumstance. Lady Isabella Hope, the wife of Governor Hope, gave her name to the wheel which is still known as The Lady Isabella. The $72^1/_2$ ft diameter wheel still stands (and turns) as a tribute to the skill of the men who worked these mines.

The wheel was built to pump water from the mines which had reached a depth of 200 fathoms. This was carried out by a series of pumps in the Engine Shaft, to which the wheel was connected by a "rod duct" of graceful stone arches carrying a connecting rod on a series of rollers which converted the wheel's motion into a vertical reciprocating movement through a huge "T" rocker beam.

There are a number of similar "T"

rockers located down the shaft to the 235 fathom level, connected to the near vertical operating rod which worked the pumps which lifted water through a series of sumps to the main adit level which is described later.

The water ran out along the adit to discharge into the Laxey river. Follow *Walk 2* to the Laxey Wheel and walk up to the Engine Shaft and ponder the weights involved and imagine how those miners handled the heavy timbers and castings, lowered them down the shaft and assembled them underground with little or no light. Thanks to the careful restoration work which has been carried out in recent years, it is sometimes possible to see the wheel turn and drive the great connecting rods.

The author investigates copper staining at North Bradda

There were seven main shafts at Laxey, the oldest of which was the Engine Shaft commenced in 1824 and reaching a depth of 247 fathoms below adit level. Dumbells, the main shaft, was commenced in the early 1850s and reached 302 fathoms, deeper than any other at Laxey.

The underground galleries at Laxey extend $1\frac{1}{4}$ miles to end well up the valley under Agneash village. Levels were driven every ten fathoms and all of the shafts were connected, but not at every level. Most of the workings were dug in slate but difficult dykes of granite were encountered throughout the mine.

There are many interesting surface remains at Laxey, of which the world-famous wheel is without doubt the most dominant. What is not so well known, but in many ways more interesting, is

the "man engine" situated below the surface in the Welch shaft. This was a water pressure engine with a 12ft stroke which was installed in 1881 and was connected to a rod which descended the shaft to at least the 200 fathom level. The rod was made up from 10 x 7-inch baulks of timber connected by iron straps and supported by large iron rollers. The tremendous weight of the rod was counterbalanced by three "T" rockers and ballast boxes. Miners used the man engine to climb and descend the mine by stepping on and off iron platforms fixed to both sides of the rod every 12ft, matching the stroke of the pressure engine, and corresponding with platforms on the side of the shaft. It took a miner 25 minutes to reach adit level from the 200 fathom level — almost twice as quick as the alternative which was to climb the ladders.

It is hard to imagine the working conditions in which men had to climb down ladders 1,200 ft, do a day's work and then climb back up again — and repeat it six days a week! The only light that the miner had to work with was a candle stuck in a lump of clay on his hat. It almost defies belief.

The Laxey vein was worked further up the valley under the shadow of Snaefell by the same company. The Great Snaefell Mine is described in more detail in *Manx Meander, stage 2,* as is the North Laxey Mine which represents the northernmost extremity to which the Laxey vein was worked.

The demise of the Manx mines led to the extensive emigration of Manx miners in search of gold in Australia, South Africa and North America.

Quarries

Before leaving the extractive industries, mention should be made of the various quarries around the island. From the early part of the 18th century, each parish had quarries from which slate was taken for building.

In 1713, Tynwald, the island's Parliament introduced the first Highway Act, appointed an Overseer of Highways and placed an onus of repair on landowners.

This, coupled with the Boundary Walls Act of 1713, increased the demand for stone. The large quarries at Douglas, Ramsey and Peel provided building materials for the developing towns.

Quarries were developed for roofing slate at Peel and South Barrule and perhaps some of the largest workings were to be found at Glen Rushen and Sulby Glen where levels and inclines can still be seen. Despite a great deal of expense in opening these quarries in search of good slate, none was found suitable for export in the way Welsh slate was.

Limestone has always been quarried in the south of the island, with some very old workings and limekilns at Ballahot and Ballasalla. Much of Castletown, including the castle, was built from limestone and there are disused quarries at Scarlett from where most of that stone was won.

A number of clay pits were dug at various times for brick production. The two most significant sites were at Ballacorey — where a bright red brick was produced from boulder clay — and at Glenfaba, where a slaty clay produced many thousands of common bricks which were fired at Peel, near the power station. That operation only ceased within the last decade, the production of concrete bricks hastening the demise of the traditional clay brick.

The old Snaefell Mines which are visited on Stage 2 of the Manx Meander

Farming and fishing

Of the other Manx industries, farming has the longest history, having been practised for around 4,000 years, as witnessed by evidence from the Meayl Circle at Cregneash, described in the previous chapter, where the builders are known to have cultivated some form of wheat.

Today, agriculture is relatively unimportant to the Manx economy, being responsible — with forestry and fishing — for only about three per cent of the gross national product by the late 1970s.

A recognition of the suitability of the island's climate and soil to the cultivation of grass has led to a general increase in grazing land at the expense of arable farming. This is now concentrated on land below 600ft in the southern and northern lowlands and the east and west coastal plateaux.

21

The decline of mining and other industries led to the depopulation of higher lands where the inhabitants often led a crofting lifestyle, with residents also working in the mines or the fishing industry. Abandoned fields and ruined houses can be seen on higher land in many parts of the island.

The move towards mixed farming and grazing has brought a parallel increase in the number of sheep on the Isle of Man, which now outnumber people by about two to one. Some of their wool is used at mills at Laxey and St John in the production of Manx tweed, whose colours are intended to reflect those of the Manx landscape. Imported breeds have replaced the small, but hardy, native Manx Loaghtan with its four or six horns. As with other upland areas in the British Isles, Manx sheep farmers suffered severe restrictions on the sale of their sheep following the Chernobyl nuclear accident.

The part-time nature of the Manx fisherman's work was in part responsible for the industry's decline. In 1864, the herring industry employed nearly 300 boats and 2,800 men. By 1939, the numbers had shrunk to nine and 47.

Today, relatively few of the boats to be seen in the island's fishing ports are Manx owned, although fishing for shellfish — chiefly escallops and queenies — for export has grown in importance, with an estimated £1/2m-worth of shellfish, caught by about 40 boats, exported annually during the 1970s. The island's most famous fish product remains its smoked herring, and the place to get your freshly smoked Manx kippers is at one of the kipperies by the harbour at Peel.

Industry today

The importance of tourism to the Manx economy remains significant, although the Tourist Department sees a more sophisticated visitor — in search of the beautiful landscape and the island's rich past, and perhaps enjoying the second or third holiday of a year — replacing the old bucket-and-spade brigade. The TT Races, of course, continue to attract huge numbers of motorcycle devotees for a fortnight which knows no parallel as many of the island's roads become a giant race track.

But today, tourism is only the third most important industry, after the financial sector and manufacturing. The island's original manufacturing industries were associated with the needs of other local industries and included sail-making. Herring nets were made in small factories in Peel and Port St Mary and boatbuilding and its associated trades were also important.

The decline of these industries led to an imbalance in the Manx economy and so, from the 1950s, Government attention was directed to the encouragement of new industries, including textiles and light engineering.

Today, the main concentrations of industry are on trading estates, particularly at Douglas, at Ronaldsway airport, and at Jurby airfield in the north of the island, where one company has been working on an ambitious airship project for some years.

Against the high cost of raw materials and transport, Manx industry must weigh the liberal tax régime and relatively low labour costs. A debate continues to rage as to whether the island should sever its common VAT arrangement with the UK. This would benefit the tourist industry by enabling goods and services to be offered at lower prices, but would bring new, expensive and time-consuming restrictions for the exporters of manufactured goods. ❏

Railway history

Isle of Man Railways locomotives Fenella and Mona double-heading on the now closed Peel line at Ballacarry

THE Victorians described the Isle of Man as "the gem of the Irish Sea". And well they might, for it was they who developed it as a popular watering place. The island became the playground of north west England, served by a comprehensive network of sea routes by which thousands of people travelled for their summer holidays. If Blackpool was the Costa del Sol, then the Isle of Man was the Majorca of the period.

The surviving rail and tram networks on the island owe their existence to this holiday trade and they provide the public transport back-up for the walks in this book.

It is perhaps hard to imagine now, but travel between the towns and villages of the Isle of Man was extremely arduous in the middle of the last century. Castletown was still the island's capital, but Douglas was expanding rapidly as a centre of culture and trade attracting merchants and gentry. It became a focus for smuggling, particularly of tobacco, brandy and rum, thanks to advantageous rates of taxes payable to the Lord of Mann, compared with the rates prevailing in England.

The difficulty of communication is witnessed by an account of a fire at King William's College in 1844, to which a battalion of men was sent from the castle in nearby Castletown. The fire was intense and a messenger was sent on horseback to Douglas to summon the fire engine. The engine was immediately despatched to Castletown but took almost six hours to travel the 12 miles, because of the condition of the largely unsurfaced roads. More roads were laid out by the Disafforesting Commissioners in 1860 and many of these form the basis of the present network. It was not until 1923 that any significant improvement in the running surfaces of the rural roads was made — considerably later than in the rest of the British Isles, with the possible exception of Ireland and the remoter parts of Scotland.

Railway mania

It is not surprising, given the state of the island's roads, that when "railway mania" hit Britain there was also considerable interest in the promotion of a number of railways in the Isle of Man. Many of these early schemes came to nothing, but in 1870 the Isle of Man Railway Company was formed.

The company promoted the building of 3ft gauge lines to connect Douglas to Castletown, Peel and Ramsey. But with a registered capital of £200,000 and only £30,000 subscribed by 1872, there were problems. The idea of a line to Ramsey was dropped and, under the guidance of Sir John Pender and the Duke of Sutherland — who became Chairman in 1872 — the company gained in strength and stature.

Work was commenced on the line from Douglas to Peel and the first train ran on May 1, 1873, hauled by a 2-4-0 tank engine, *Sutherland*, built that year by Beyer Peacock of Manchester. It was the forerunner of a successful class of engine which has provided faithful service right up to the present day, and this particular locomotive can still be seen in the Steam Railway Museum at Port Erin.

While the Peel line flourished, work continued on the line to serve the south of the island and this was completed the following year and opened to traffic in August, 1874, from Douglas to Port Erin. The company by this time operated five locomotives and 50 coaches and wagons.

By 1870, the island had entered a period of rapid expansion and most of the hotels that now form the façade of Douglas Promenade were built between this date and 1900 to cater for the rapid rise in holiday traffic. By 1890 the trade had reached 275,500 people a year.

Ramsey felt badly done by, having been left out of the Isle of Man Railway Company's plans. Not surprisingly, a group of distinguished gentlemen with interests in Ramsey and the north of the island promoted the Manx Northern Railway Company Limited, registered in 1877 with a capital of £90,000 — this too proved a difficult sum to raise.

However, the financial goal was reached and in September, 1879, the first train entered service with little or no celebration. The line had been con-

IMR No. 13, Kissack, at Santon station

MER car No. 20 at Ballure, approaching Ramsey

structed between Ramsey and St John's, where a terminus was built adjoining the Isle of Man Railway Company halt. There was a physical connection to the Peel to Douglas line, but the Manx Northern enjoyed no running rights over Isle of Man Railway Company metals.

By 1880, the Manx Northern had also built a tramway from its station at Ramsey to serve the harbour. The company at this time operated three locomotives. The first two were built by Sharp Stewart and Company Limited, and the third by Beyer Peacock to exactly the same design as the IMR engines. At this time only the latter carried a name, *Thornhill*. The two earlier engines were named *Ramsey* and *Northern* in 1893.

The Foxdale mines, which were among the most productive of any in the British Isles, were a potentially lucrative goal for both the IMR and MNR. The Manx Northern had the advantage with its quayside tramway, but the ore had to be moved by cart to St John's for

onward shipment and competition was fierce. Both companies wanted to build a branch line to Foxdale.

In the end a new company was to build the two-and-a-half-mile line between Foxdale and the MNR line at St John's — the Foxdale Railway Company. The construction work was completed, albeit with some difficulty, and an agreement was entered into whereby the MNR undertook to operate the service. This peculiar arrangement was to lead eventually to the downfall of the Manx Northern, but not before the arrival of the largest locomotive ever to operate on the island's railways. The six-coupled locomotive, MNR No.4, *Caledonia*, built by Dubs and Company, was required to handle the heavy freight traffic on the predominantly 1:50 gradient of the Foxdale line. This locomotive, too, can be seen at the Port Erin Museum.

All this activity made St John's the Crewe Junction of the Isle of Man, but apart from the former Manx Northern

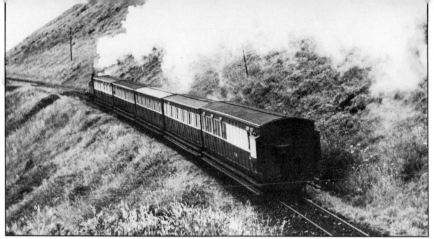

IMR No. 5, Mona, on the exposed Ramsey line at Gob y Deigan — in the days of MNR operation, rolling stock was turned round to prevent uneven weathering

station building — which is now a private house — little remains to give a clue to the bustling activity of St John's in its heyday.

In 1905, the whole of the steam railway network was taken over by the Isle of Man Railway Company on the authority of the Manx Government.

One other branch line remained to be built. During the 1914-18 war, a camp was built at Knockaloe, south of Peel, to house some 20,000 internees and a branch line to serve it was constructed from a junction near Glenfaba Mill approximately one mile away. There was an associated siding on Peel Quay. The whole branch was built for the British Government and was completely removed on cessation of hostilities. The severe gradient of the 1:20 branch meant that it was exclusively worked by *Caledonia*.

IMR crest as featured on locomotives

The tourist trade picked up again after the first world war, but the railway found itself in increasing competition with the motor coach.

Motor bus operations had been introduced within the Borough of Douglas by the Corporation in 1914, with a 25-seat Straker Squire omnibus. After the war, it expanded the fleet with a number of Tilling-Stevens petrol-electric omnibuses.

The first serious bus service outside Douglas was introduced in 1927 in the form of Manxland Bus Services Ltd, which had a strong connection with Cumberland Motor Services Ltd. The rural roads of the island were by this time being greatly improved and surfaced with tar and chippings. Concerned at this potential competitor operating 14 ADC 28-seater buses, the Isle of Man Railway Company took an interest in forming a consortium with other local operators, and Manx Motors Ltd was formed, operating eight Thornycroft buses. The railway responded by operating 100 trains a day. It now had 16 locomotives available, although in reality was only operating 14 in regular service. The railway company had acquired its last and largest Beyer Peacock locomotive in 1926, still in 2-4-0 format and named *Mannin*. It was built specially for the Port Erin line and was designed as a more powerful engine to reduce the need for banking, or double-heading, on the climb out of Douglas through the Nunnery cutting, or on the bank out of Ballasalla on the return journey.

The Manxland venture eventually went into liquidation, having made the mistake of underestimating the seasonal nature of the island traffic. In the meantime, the IMR had formed yet another company, Isle of Man Road Services Ltd, operating the fastest vehicles which were 28-seater Thornycroft BC omnibuses

The Isle of Man Railway Company — operating its train services to capacity at cut price fares and also a faster, more efficient bus service — saw off the other bus competitors by 1930. This monopoly eventually was to work to the detriment of the railway but, up to the outbreak of the second world war, was to guarantee a period of stability and consolidation of the IMR interests.

The age of the tram

The second world war was to see many changes on the island — but, in parallel with the development of the steam railways, the Isle of Man had also seen the rise of various tram systems, many of which survive today in their original glory.

The year 1870 was a significant one in the history of the development of Douglas and many decisions were taken which would shape the town which is now the island's modern capital. Victoria Street was completed in 1875, having cut through much of old Douglas in the process. It joined a new promenade which was opened the same year by Governor Henry Loch and still bears his name. The Loch Promenade was not completed until 1877 but it dramatically pushed the sea wall some 300ft to seaward, enabling the building of the grand façade of Victorian hotels and boarding houses.

Thomas Lightfoot, a retired civil engineering contractor, saw his opportunity with this new promenade and promoted his ideas for a horse tramway along the full span of Douglas Bay. By

1876, the Douglas Horse Tramway was partially completed and two trams were in operation carrying fare-paying passengers. The line was completed in January 1877 and still runs today. The 3ft gauge tramway has been altered on a number of occasions to meet the development of the town but generally follows the original concept.

The tramway changed hands, eventually being purchased by the Isle of Man Tramways and Electric Power Company Limited in 1894. The directors of this company, having seen the success of the horse tramway, were keen to extend their tramway operations to serve the upper parts of the town which were now being developed. Horse traction was not practical because of the steep gradients so they proposed a cable-drawn tramway.

In this system, the trams were drawn by a continuous cable beneath the road surface, traction was controlled by a "gripper" on each tram, clasping the moving cable. A similar system still operates in San Francisco.

By August 1896 the one-and-a-half-mile tramway had been laid from the Salisbury Hotel up Victoria Street, Prospect Hill, Bucks Road, Woodbourne Road, York Road and Broadway. A winding house and car shed were built at York Road to accommodate 15 cars. A full day was taken to thread the cable using two traction engines and the two ends were joined in an 80ft splice.

In 1902, the horse tramway and the cable tramway were purchased by the Douglas Corporation. They both ran as a municipal undertaking, being supplemented by buses in 1914. By 1920, buses were operating on the Upper Douglas routes and by 1929 the cable cars were withdrawn and the York Road depot became the bus garage and workshops.

Sadly, nothing remains of the cable tramway, the depot being demolished in 1989 to make way for housing. Some

DON'T · LEAVE · OUR · ISLAND
WITHOUT · SEEING · IT · !

16 MILES OF BREATHTAKING COUNTRYSIDE

CLIMB 2,036 FEET TO THE TOP OF SNAEFELL

17 MILES OF BEAUTIFUL COASTLINE

2 MILES CLIP CLOP ALONG THE PROMENADE

Discover and enjoy the Island, take a train, tram or bus and let the driver take the strain.

Tickets are available from either of the Tourist Information Centres, at Sefton Buildings or the Sea Terminal, Douglas, Tel. 686766. Also at all Bus and Railway Stations.

THE · ISLE OF · MAN
DEPARTMENT OF TOURISM AND TRANSPORT

The harbour front at Douglas, near the terminus of the steam railway

diverter pulleys remain buried under the roadway and emerge from time to time during roadworks. Two cars survived as a summer bungalow at the Lhen, each with one side dismantled. One car was subsequently restored and now forms an exhibit at the horse tramway depot at Strathallan Crescent in Douglas — *see Douglas Town Trail.*

In 1891 a scheme was promoted to build a marine drive from Douglas, south to Port Soderick. The company formed to undertake this ambitious project suffered financial and other setbacks, but by persistence the scheme developed and eventually incorporated a tramway.

Douglas Southern Electric Tramways was incorporated as a limited company in 1895. By 1896 a standard (4ft $8^1/_2$ins) gauge line had been laid, crossing three major bridges and several half-bridges. A generating station was built at Pigeon Stream to provide electric power at 550V DC for the 12 double-deck cars, six of them fitted with motors.

The crimson and white livery must have presented an attractive sight on the Marine Drive. Four additional trailer cars were provided by Brush Electrical Engineering Company in 1897 and two of these were converted to power cars at the tramway workshops at Little Ness.

Nothing remains of the tramway, which closed in 1939, except the toll gate house and the odd metal sleeper. The sites of various points of interest are described in *Walk 5*.

The depot trackwork was removed to the National Tramway Museum, at Crich, Derbyshire, in 1960, where car No. 1 remains preserved.

Redevelopment is nothing new and today's changes on the Isle of Man pale into insignificance against the background of the speculative ventures of the last quarter of the 19th century. The Howstrake Estate, near Douglas, was being developed to provide housing on a grand scale and to open up access to this, new roads had to be built. The Douglas Bay Estate Limited, with several shareholders and directors common to the Douglas Horse Tramway, started work in 1882 on building a new coast road from Derby Castle northwards towards Groudle.

By 1893, Port e Vada creek had been filled in and a single line tramway of 3ft gauge had been laid as far as Groudle Glen where a new hotel was built. An electricity generating station and car sheds were built at Port e Vada and occupy the same site today. In the same year, the Douglas and Laxey Coast Electric Tramway Company was formed and soon acquired the Howstrake Tramway. By July 1894 trams were running to Laxey.

MER crew break at Laxey

The company acquired the Douglas horse tramway in the same year and changed its name to Isle of Man Tramways and Electric Power Company Limited. It also embarked on a policy of selling electric power as a "side line". It was 1899 before the tramway reached Ramsey with its double track on the same alignment that exists to the present day. Additional depots were built at Laxey and Ramsey and another power station at Laxey. A final power station was completed in 1898, at Ballaglass $12^1/_2$ miles from Douglas.

All of the original rolling stock is still in use today, with the exception of those damaged and destroyed in a fire at the Laxey Depot in 1930.

The tramways of the island had been financed by underwritings from Dumbell's Bank. There was a financial involvement between the individual directors of the bank and the tramways which led to the collapse of the former. The tramway was rescued from receivership in 1902 by a new company, the Manx Electric Railway Company Limited.

In 1895, a 3ft 6ins gauge tramway was built from Laxey to the top of Snaefell, the highest point on the island. The tramway was almost five miles long and had its own power station about half way between Laxey and the summit. The Manx Northern Railway locomotive *Caledonia* was hired to haul the construction trains, running on a temporary third rail laid to the 3ft gauge.

The original rolling stock of six cars, built by Milnes of Birkenhead, still exist and are housed in the original depot at Laxey. One of the cars, No. 5, was rebuilt, following a fire, in 1971.

The cars collect current from the overhead supply by Hopkinson rigid bow collectors. The centre rail is purely to guide the tram bogies, although originally intended for braking on the descent, using a form of calliper brakes operated by the brakesman.

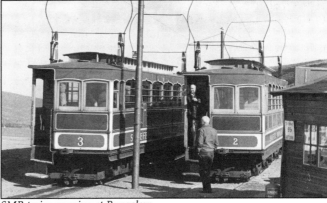

SMR trains crossing at Bungalow

These are still retained for use in emergency but all the tram cars were fitted with a new rheostatic (electric) main braking system in 1977, using secondhand equipment from a number of German tramcars purchased from Aachen. Traction is by ordinary adhesion (there is no rack and pinion system as in some mountain railways) and the average gradient of the line is 1 in 12.

The railway network today

Although the advent of the second world war stopped the holiday traffic overnight there was to be an unexpected bonus for the Isle of Man Railway, moving internees who were billeted in requisitioned boarding houses in all of the island's towns, with corresponding movement of troops. Material from the Foxdale mines spoil heaps was moved to provide infill for new airfields.

The Manx Electric Railway was less fortunate, picking up little wartime trade, although mines spoil was also taken from Laxey to Ramsey as hardcore for runways at Jurby and Andreas airfields. This followed a disastrous period — not only had the 1930 fire at Laxey destroyed four power cars and seven trailers, but a flood later in the year hit the Laxey power station, also causing additional damage in the lower part of the village for which the company was held liable.

The island enjoyed a post-war boom in holiday trade, but it was short lived and by 1950 decline had set in. The Manx Electric Railway, still smarting from the pre-war problems and suffering from lack of maintenance, came near to liquidation. It was finally rescued by the Isle of Man Government in 1957.

The Isle of Man Railway was not so fortunate. Losses, coupled with competition from its own subsidiary bus company and the advent of the ubiquitous motor car, led to winter closures in the early 1960s on the Peel and Ramsey lines.

With only eight locomotives available for work, even maintaining the service became a problem. The end was in sight and 1966 appeared to signal liquidation. Train operations ceased but there was a slight reprieve when the railway was operated by a private consortium aided by a tourism grant. Eventually this was to fail and rails were removed from the Foxdale, Peel and Ramsey lines. During this demolition work, sparks from oxy-acetylene burners set fire to the carriage sheds at St John's and many irreplaceable coaches were destroyed.

Then the Isle of Man Government stepped in and purchased the remain-

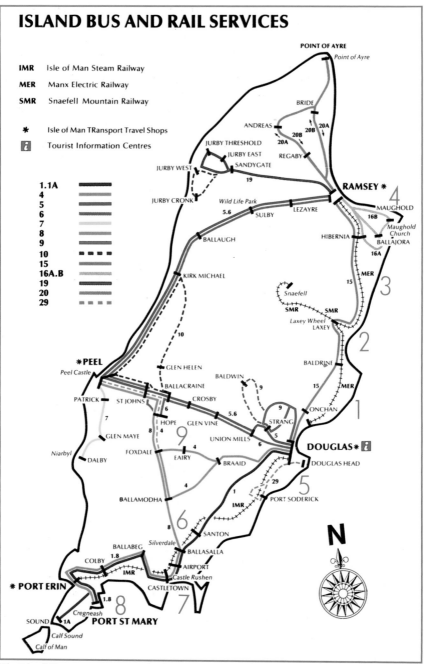

The Isle of Man transport network. The large numbers in magenta relate to the short walks and excursions in the following section

ing railway lands and the Port Erin line, which has been protected to the present day.

The Manx Electric Railway, Snaefell Mountain Railway and the Steam Railway are all operated by the Transport Division of the Isle of Man Department of Tourism and Transport — as is the fleet of modern buses.

See also the Groudle Glen Railway — Walk 1.

Other railways

A number of contractors' tramways were built on the island in connection with major civil engineering works and, although well documented, there are no remains other than bits of track formation here and there.

Without doubt, the most interesting of these was the Port Erin Harbour Tramway which saw the first steam locomotive in the Isle of Man. The island's Harbour Commissioners engaged Sir John Coode, an eminent civil engineer, to design a breakwater to create a harbour of refuge at Port Erin and provide shelter from westerly gales. Work began in 1864 and the Commissioners acquired a secondhand locomotive, three steam cranes and a number of wagons all to a gauge of 7ft. Built in 1853 by Wilson and Company of Leeds, the 0-4-0 locomotive was named after Henry B Loch, the Governor who was responsible for many of the development schemes in the latter half of the 19th century.

The tramway served the block-making yard, a quarry and the breakwater. The site of the quarry is readily seen behind the marine biological station — *see Manx Meander, stage 7.*

In 1899 the Douglas Corporation began work on a new reservoir at Injebreck at West Baldwin. A tramway was built to a gauge of 3ft, and it eventually reached a length of five miles. Traces of the trackbed can be seen alongside the River Glass from the West Baldwin road. Four saddle tank engines

were used during the six-year construction contract.

At Poortown Quarry, near Peel, the island's Highways Committee operated a quarry to provide crushed granite roadstone to parish foremen by means of the Manx Northern and, later, the Isle of Man Railway. A gravity-operated 2ft gauge tramway ran from the quarry to St Germain's halt alongside the road. The empty trucks were brought back to the quarry by horse. The line of the tramway has recently been obliterated by a new footpath but it is possible to see where it curved onto the loading bay which is still in place.

The Abbey Clay Works, near St John's, had a tramway connecting the Clay Pit at Ballaharra to the works which produced tiles. The tramway ran on top of an embankment which can still be seen.

The remains of a number of cliff lifts can also still be seen around the island and some of them are described in the walks which follow.

Mine tramways

Moving the ore within the Isle of Man's mines and their immediate surroundings involved tramways of various sorts, of which very little remains today.

The earliest seem to have been wooden tram roads on which wheeled buckets were pushed by the miners. Traces of wooden ways have been found in the oldest mine workings, at Bradda, near Port Erin, which were probably in use in the middle of the 19th century, as — by 1903 — work in the North Bradda Mine had almost ceased. There is no doubt that some form of timber ways were also used in the Foxdale Mines.

It is to the Laxey Mines that we turn for the most extensive tramway, and, because the mines were worked until 1929, its history is well documented — *see Walk 2.* ❏

Short walks and trips

THIS section of the book features a series of relatively easy excursions, using the Manx public transport system to reach places of interest. Most of the walks are between two and four miles long and are aimed particularly at parties with children. Refreshment facilities are usually close at hand. The section opens with a series of heritage trails based on the four principal towns of the island, and intended to complement "official" trails which are available for Peel, Ramsey and Castletown. The locations of the other nine walks are shown on the map on page 32.

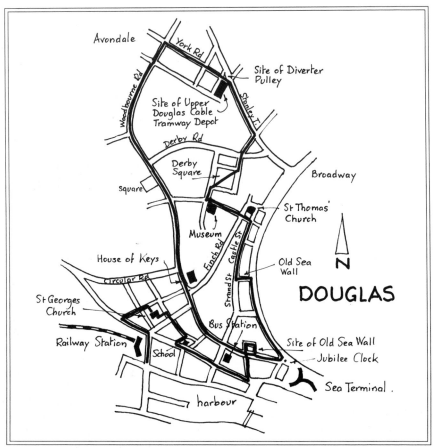

Douglas Town Trail map — see facing page

Douglas town trail

This tour of the modern capital of the Isle of Man seeks out its more historic quarters that have survived the recent redevelopment boom. It focuses particularly on the route of the old cable tramway

The broad sweep of Douglas Promenade — note the sunken gardens on the right, near the southern end of Douglas Bay

OUR walk around Douglas begins outside the main entrance of the Steam Railway Station.

Douglas has not always been the island's capital, having only replaced Castletown in 1869. Douglas grew around the mouth of the river from which it took its name. Look down the harbour from the station and imagine standing on a salt marsh with just a few houses to your left and a few small boats pulled up on the grass — that would have been all there was to see of Douglas a few hundred years ago.

Douglas has continued to change since then and there is no doubt that the Victorians have had the biggest say in this respect... until the 1980s, that is. Now, hardly a day goes by without some part of Douglas and its history being demolished to make way for "progress".

To start our walk we shall go up Bank Hill alongside the railway station buildings. Reflect a while on the size of the station buildings and their ornamental gates. These impressive structures were built between 1885 and 1892 to serve a narrow gauge network of railways on the island, but they would have done a major railway company in Britain proud. Their grandeur reflects the importance that the Isle of Man Railway had within the island. Turning left at the top of the hill, we walk a short distance up Peel Road before turning right into Hope Street. Most of the houses in this street date from 1850 and marked the limits of Upper Douglas at the time. They were the residences of the gentry and merchants and most remain to this day as private houses. After crossing St George's Street, we stay on the right hand side of the street and enter St George's churchyard through the side door.

Although Douglas is mostly in the parish of Onchan, St George's has always been the principal church in the town. There has been a church on this site since early Christian times, although the present building dates only from 1848.

As you walk down the path towards the church, you will notice on the left some plain wooden crosses in a grassed area of the churchyard marking the site of the graves of cholera victims. Beside the main entrance to the church is a memorial stone surrounded by iron railings which describes the plague epidemic which struck Douglas in 1832.

On the way out of the churchyard through the main gates you will pass the tomb of Sir William Hillary, founder of the Royal National Lifeboat Institution (see also Walk 5).

Turn right on leaving the church and walk down Upper Church Street, crossing Athol Street, now the main business centre of the town. This originally contained the residences of professionals and merchants, and many of their houses can still be seen amid the new development. We continue down Church Street, past the Courthouse and, as we approach the junction with John Street, we pass some of the oldest buildings in the town, now occupied by shops and a bistro. Ahead of us is the Town Hall, built in 1899 when the town received its municipal status and became a Borough. If you

look carefully, you will see where the first fire station was located.

We continue our meander, turning right by the multi-storey car park and passing the former Barrack Street Mission Hall, another remnant of old Douglas, now tastefully converted into a wine bar and discothèque.

The next building was originally built as a school and if you look carefully as we walk down Hanover Street, you will see its foundation stone, proclaiming that "this stone was laid by Mrs George A Ring on July 4, 1888". The school was to revolutionise education in Douglas and was one of the first Board Schools, a fact nobly proclaimed in the elaborate brickwork on the main chimney stack fronting Lord Street. George Ring was the Manx Attorney General and Chairman of the newly constituted Board of Education.

We continue to walk along, passing Coronation Terrace and the bus station to turn left up Fort Street, passing the Isle of Man Steam Packet Company's engineering works and boilermakers' shop.

The area on our left and that embraced by the bus station was the heart of old Douglas. It has long been changed, although only recently has Seneschal House been demolished. This was the building in which the first Town Commissioners met in 1860. Also now gone is St Barnabas Church, in which I was christened, not, I hasten to add, in 1860.

The original hospital and dispensary for Douglas was, until 1886, on the seaward side of Fort Street and the wall at the rear of these premises was the sea wall, of which a remnant still exists as I write this text. But I am sure that by the time you read this book the whole lot could be demolished. If the Villiers car park is still there when you get to Victoria Street, cross over and continue up Fort Street as far as you can and as you walk around the limits of the car park look up at the building at the end of the yard and you will clearly see the stone sea wall.

That circuit of a not very salubrious part of Douglas brings us back into Victoria Street, opposite the former Salisbury Hotel, which is now the headquar-ters of Isle of

Victoria Street, 1896 — the cable tramway under construction

Man Breweries Ltd. The building has been renovated and has a fine example of a Victorian stucco façade

This is almost the terminus of the Upper Douglas Cable Tramway. The actual terminus was near the Jubilee Clock so it is probably worth strolling up to it and starting in earnest from there to follow the line of the tramway which was built in 1896 and pulled up in 1930.

The twin tracks of the tramway ran each side of Victoria Street, which — as you can see — is changing dramatically. Rounding the bend at the top of Victoria Street, the tramway climbed Prospect Hill, passing what was Dumbell's Bank, now NatWest, which was entwined in the financing of the several tramways built in the island. It was this involvement, through its directors, which led to the bank's downfall and much hardship to many local people (further reading of The Dumbell Affair by Connery Chappell, published by Stephenson, is recommended). While the left hand side of Prospect Hill has changed little, the right hand side has altered dramatically.

The tracks required more clearance on the Prospect Hill corner between the up and the down line but they still

straddled the middle of the road.

Continuing up the hill, we approach the imposing Government office building on the corner of Finch Road, which — when the tramway was built — was the headquarters of the Bank of Mona. It was at this point that the two tracks diverged to the kerbside to continue up Bucks Road. We pass Tynwald chambers where the Keys, Legislative Council and Tynwald sit to conduct their business. Alongside, in a modern building, are housed the administrative functions of many of the departments of Government. Opposite is the splendid Roman Catholic church of St Mary.

Bucks Road has much the same appearance architecturally as it did in the days of the tramway — if you look beyond the razzamatazz of today's lifestyle. Look at the ornate gargoyles on the tower of Finch Hill United Reform Church. At Rosemount, Trinity Church is worth a close inspection to admire its elegant pseudo-Gothic style. Its tall, slender spire is a prominent landmark and, to my mind, it is the pick of the town's churches. The Rosemount Hotel opposite is a good place to stop for refreshment as we are almost half way through our walk.

Cable car No.73 at Avondale Corner — open country when the tramway opened

When the tramway reached Woodbourne Road, there was sporadic development to Avondale Corner, at York Road. The tramway promoters recognised that Douglas would expand and were brave in taking their tramway into what were clearly, at that time, open fields. I wonder what they would think if they could see the area now. I suspect they would not be surprised — they were extremely far-sighted entrepreneurs.

If you look at the larger properties built in Woodbourne Road you will see that this was definitely where the wealthy people of Douglas chose to live and the area soon became Upper Douglas.

If you look through the gate of the Masonic Buildings you will be able to make out Woodbourne House, just visible at the rear of the main building, and it was from this estate that most of what we know as Upper Douglas was developed.

A superb job was done, with wonderful squares built around ornamental parks, giving us today little havens of peace to sit and take the sun, watch the birds or do nothing. It is a pity that more people do not realise their value.

We pass close by Woodbourne Square gardens and, behind the Masonic Buildings, we can see Hilary Park just a little off our route.

Back to the tramway — as it approached Avondale Corner, identified by the second set of traffic lights we have passed, the twin tracks merged to a single line just after the corner and descended York Road to the depot and then continued to Broadway and the Promenade.

The depot and the engine room has only recently been demolished to make way for more housing. It was located opposite the ornamental triangular gardens at the junction of York Road and Ballaquayle Road. The four tracks in the depot building were accessed by a Y-junction and a traverser. The cable came from the winding house along a tunnel, part of which remains under the road, and the cable changed direction via a number of large pulleys located in a diverter pit which is just below a grating in the footway by the garden.

The tramway continued on into Ballaquayle Road as a single track, apart from a short double section across the frontage of the depot. The single line ran straight down Ballaquayle Road and Broadway to the Promenade but, by 1901, the steepness of the gradient and the number of curves, together with friction on the cable in the passing places, made it almost impossible to work the lower section. In 1902, the lower section was abandoned and the terminus on this leg was moved to Stanley View.

We follow the tramway down Ballaquayle Road to Stanley View and leave its route to return to our starting point, turning right into Glen Falcon Road, and passing the Glen Falcon Brewery, which is one of the bastions of "real ale". We cross Derby Road into Derby Square and enter the garden in the centre of the Square to cross it diagonally.

As we go into the gardens, look across at the bronze statue on the right. This is one of 23 bronzes cast from the famous sculpture, *The Kiss*, by Auguste Rodin, the celebrated French sculptor.

We leave the garden by the top gate on Albion Terrace. A fine old terrace has recently been demolished to make way for a modern elderly persons' home, but some idea of the style of the buildings in this part of Douglas can be seen in Cambridge and Osborne Terraces, which bring us conveniently to the Manx Museum situated at the top of Crellin's Hill.

The original building, with its ornate central tower, was built as a hospital to replace the earlier one in Fort Street, and the foundation stone was laid in 1886 by Rebecca Noble, the wife of Henry Bloom Noble, a wealthy philanthropist and public figure. By 1929, even this hospital was insufficient for the needs of the town and was replaced by a building on the present hospital site at Westmoreland Road and the building became the National Museum. The new extension was completed in 1989 and opened by HM the Queen.

The museum houses a wide variety of exhibits, with modern displays of Manx history, archaeology, natural history, and folk life, as well as an art gallery. The museum also houses the Manx National Reference Library.

We now go down Crellin's Hill, passing St Thomas's church and school, into Castle Street and Strand Street as far as Howard Street, where we shall go out

The Tower of Refuge

onto the promenade. Strand Street is now entering a period of change and much of the old façade will go. It was originally named Sand Street and again we have to imagine that, originally, all of the houses backed straight onto the sea. Indeed, as we approach the Loch Parade church in Howard Street, look to the left up the back lane and you will again see a remnant of the old sea wall.

Once on the promenade, the Tower of Refuge — built in 1832 at the instigation of Sir William Hillary, founder of the RNLI — can be seen on St Mary's Rock

A tram driver's eye view of Douglas promenade

in the middle of Douglas Bay. Sir William was impressed to promote the building of the castellated tower following the wreck in 1830 of the steamer St George after it struck the rocks. Sir William gained a second gold medal from the institution for his part in the ensuing rescue.

We walk towards the Sea Terminal along the Loch Promenade, admiring the Victorian façade of the hotels and boarding houses built after the new promenade was completed in 1877. The sea wall was more or less on the line of the footway on the opposite side of the present road. In 1934 the sunken gardens and promenade walkway were built, creating the promenade as we see it today.

As you can see, however, time and tide wait for no-one, as, at the time of writing, the whole of the area occupied by the Villiers Hotel and adjoining properties was destined for redevelopment.

We are now back to the Jubilee Clock in Victoria Street and more or less where we started from. Other tramway and related relics in Douglas are described in other walks. ❏

Peel city trail

This tour of the Isle of Man's only "city" includes a visit to the richly historic islet where the early Norse Kings of Mann held sway

The ruins of St German's Cathedral on St Patrick's Isle, Peel

PEEL (*Puirt-ny-Hinshey*, in Manx) is an ancient town dating from 1582 and, like all of the principal towns in the island, it grew up around the mouth of a river. In the case of Peel, it is the river Neb, around which the town developed alongside a very substantial boat-building and fishing industry.

Today, Peel retains much of its "old-world" charm, with narrow, winding streets lined by buildings dating predominantly from the 1840s and 50s or, in some cases, the 18th century.

Our tour of Peel begins at the bus station in Athol Street. Opposite is the Royal Hotel with its old livery stables still intact and, next to it, the Athol Street Methodist Church. A little further along you will pass the entrance to the parish church of St German, built in 1884 from money collected by Bishop Hill to replace the old cathedral on Peel Island.

Strangely, it has only recently become the Cathedral of Mann, at last realising that original dream. The church was built in the English style and originally had a graceful stone spire. This was, however, damaged by a storm in 1907 and subsequently dismantled. Stones from the spire can be seen inside the entrance gates.

We continue along Athol Street to turn right into Douglas Street, after passing what were the residences of the town's gentry. From there, we walk down into Market Place. In the Square have a look in the garden embraced by the ruined church of St Peter. The clock tower with its clock donated to the town by James Kewley Ward, a native of the town and a philanthropist, who made a fortune in the timber business in America. He became Mayor of Quebec, but did not forget his birthplace, having

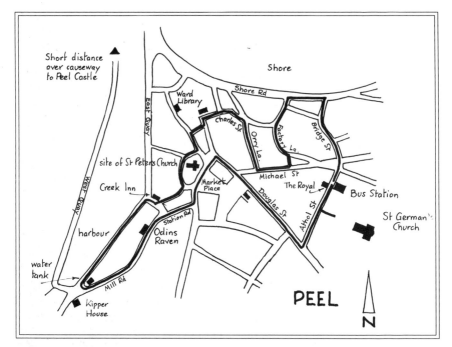

also provided the Ward Library before his death in 1910.

Continue through the Square and down Station Road, formerly Well Brow, and along Mill Road, passing the site of the old gasworks, the old railway goods shed on the right and then the fish yards and kipper houses, producing the finest Manx kippers, for which Peel is famous. In season (July to September), the whole of the harbour is covered in a haze of smoke from the oak chippings still used in the curing process. At the end of Mill Road, cross the bridge to West Quay to reach the causeway to St Patrick's Isle.

Although the castle itself is now largely ruined, it is easy to imagine why — particularly as you look down from the ramparts to the foaming Irish Sea — the island enjoyed such strategic importance.

The cathedral, also largely ruined, was built around 1390, and pre-dates most of the rest of the remains. The island has for the last few years been the scene of some

scene of some of the most exciting archaeological excavations in the British Isles and Norse and pre-Norse Celtic settlements have been uncovered. Information about some of the most exciting finds is included in Section One.

Archaeologists at work on St Patrick's Isle

After an optional stroll as far as the end of the breakwater, return along the

West Quay and over the bridge, bearing leaft along the quayside. The building opposite is one of the oldest surviving kipper houses.

The boat park on the right as we walk along the quay was the site of Peel Railway Station. There are signs of the railway presence all around, with the old water tower on the corner and the old station building now used by the Fisherman's Association. The focal point, however, is the old goods shed, now the Odin Raven boathouse, which is home for a replica of a Viking longboat which was sailed from Norway, where it was built as part of the island's Tynwald Millennium celebrations in 1979. Don't miss this opportunity to meet George, the King of the Vikings, who will be pleased to show you around.

A call at the Creek Inn for refreshment is a welcome break and most appropriate to our theme as it used to be the Railway Hotel. Then we make our way from Station Place, up Lake Lane to St Peter's Lane. Station Place itself has a place in history as it was the home of the shipbuilding yard of Harry Graves, of which more can be learned in the Leece Museum in Castle Street.

We pass behind St Peter's Church spire and can, from this angle, imagine what a beautiful church it was when it was built in the middle of the 16th century. We turn left into Castle Street — formerly Big Street, the oldest in Peel, which once had 11 public houses — and right through Love Lane into the heart of old Peel. This area was used as a barracks when the Castle was garrisoned.

Manx kippers enjoy a wide and well deserved reputation

George — "King of the Vikings"

IMR locomotive No.3, Pender, taking on water at Peel — most of the station buildings have found new uses

At the foot of Castle Street are the Ward Library and the Leece Museum (open afternoons, May to September). Eddie Leece was formerly headmaster at Peel and Chairman of the Peel Commissioners.

The trail continues from Love Lane, down Market Street, passing several

Peel's tight little streets can reveal surprising views

buildings of interest including the Mathematical School, where many famous sailors were trained.

We must be careful here at the double corner not to walk out onto the promenade but instead dodge up to the right through Charles Street, which used to be named Pilot Street, and continue uphill along Orry Lane into Michael Street, the main shopping centre of the town. You can if you wish amble up Michael Street and Athol Place to the bus station or, if you like, make another detour down Factory Lane and Beach Street to the promenade for an ice cream before returning up Bridge Street into Athol Place and the bus station.

Just to the left, off Bridge Street, is the first Wesleyan Chapel to be built on the island, in 1777, following John Wesley's first visit to Peel. It is now the home of Peel Youth Centre. ❏

Castletown town trail

One of the impressions on this circuit of the ancient capital of the Isle of Man is of the predominance of limestone in its buildings… sombre after rain, but almost white in the summer sun

WHICHEVER way you travel to Castletown, either by bus or train, Castle Rushen dominates the town and its history is very much part of the history of the island *(see History Section and the Manx Meander, stage 8).*

Castletown was formerly the capital of the island and the seat of Government until 1869, following the reforms by Governor Loch introduced in 1866. It stands on the mouth of the Silverburn river, around which the town, castle and harbour developed.

We shall start our walk in the Parade by the Doric Column which stands between the Parade and the Square and from which you will get a good view of the Castle with its curious one-fingered clock. If you read the inscriptions on the base of the column you will see that it was erected to the memory of Colonel Cornelius Smelt, who was much respected as Governor of the island and who died in 1832. However, the column never did receive his statue, which would have overlooked the Castle where he was the last Governor in residence. Subsequent Governors to 1860 resided in Lorne House, of which we may catch a glimpse in our walkabout.

The column was designed by the architect John Welch, who also designed King William's College and the Tower of Refuge in Douglas Bay. It featured an unusual sundial which was repositioned in the "glacis" of the Castle (the grass bank which once completely surrounded the castle's dry moat).

It has many faces and is supposed to tell the time by the light of the moon as well by the sun.

We shall move off with our backs to the façade of the former St Mary's church and with the Castle on our right, heading towards Arbory Street, on our left. As we leave the Square, we have to imagine that until comparatively recently, the Castle was garrisoned and the barracks were situated on our left on the site of the new municipal buildings which stand opposite the modern entrance to the Castle, through the glacis which is now the Speaker's Garden.

Much of the character of the ancient capital can be absorbed as we wander past the shops in Arbory Street until we turn right at the Crofts, which were in earlier times the residences of the wealthy merchants and professional people. It is now a very pleasant place to live and the properties are all well-maintained, preserving this corner of the island's history.

On our right is the municipal crown bowling green and adjoining tennis courts in a superbly-sheltered situation discreet within the town.

At the end of the Crofts we turn left into Malew Street, again little altered from the 19th century apart from the yellow lines! Just as Peel is predominantly sandstone, so Castletown is predominantly built from limestone. Although, when wet, it can give the town a sombre appearance, it comes alive in the bright sunlight of summer. This end of the town was the home of the artisans and evidence of workshops and builders' yards can still be seen. Pay attention here, because opposite one of those old

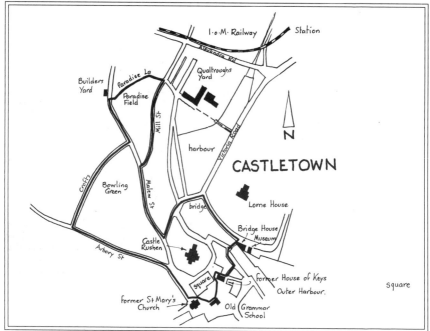

workshops we turn right up a little alley across Paradise Field to join Mill Street. On the left over the wall is the site of the old gasworks. It is only people as eccentric as me that mourn their passing.

The builders' merchant's yard opposite carries a well-known Castletown name — Qualtrough's — which is steeped in the history of the town and famous for its former boat building prowess on this site. Sir Joseph Qualtrough, the father of the present owner, was the Speaker of the House of Keys.

We are going to make our way up Mill Road back into Malew Street and continue our amble back towards the centre of the town. At the top of Bank Hill we shall turn left down to the harbour and if we look across the new development opposite, on the site of the former Castletown Brewery, we might just catch a glimpse of Lorne House, once the home of the island's Governors and now home to a computer software company.

We turn right after crossing the new bridge along Umber Quay, so called because of its association with the Ballasalla Ochre and Umber Works, and then back over the little swing bridge passing Bridge House, the former home of the Quayle family and about which you can learn more when you visit the Nautical Museum which was built in 1789.

The museum is not large, but interesting enough, as it houses the oldest surviving Manx-built vessel, *The Peggy*, a schooner-rigged armed yacht built in 1791.

On the other side of the bridge, before turning left, look at the Baillie Scott-designed police station on the corner opposite the Barbican and present entrance to the castle. As you walk along the quay, look across at Bridge House and its adjoining boathouse to see where the Peggy was built.

We turn up to the right and into Parliament Square to look at the imposing building, now a bank, which proudly

Castletown is dominated by the edifice that gives it its name

proclaims that it was once the home of the House of Keys. The Legislature sat in Castletown in this building, until 1706, when it moved to Douglas. After that, from about 1886, it became the Castletown office of Dumbell's Bank. Now, after many other different uses, the wheel has turned almost full circle.

Walking round the building, we are on the site of the very old part of the town, now demolished to make way for a car park. Preserved in the middle, fortunately, is the old Grammar School. This is the oldest intact building on the island and incorporates parts of the medieval chapel of the earlier church of St Mary built in 1698. This was replaced in 1826 by a new building, now no longer a church. We walk alongside this to enter the Parade with its Georgian-styled houses on both sides. This creates a perfect setting for many of the pageants and parades staged in the town in every summer. If you stand with your back to St Mary's Church, one of the fine terrace of houses on your left was once occupied by Captain John Quilliam who sailed under Nelson as a lieutenant on the *Victory*. After a distinguished naval career, he served wisely in Manx politics, with particular concern for the fishing industry.

Now is the time to go and see the castle. Castle Rushen dominates the town and its history is very much part of the history of the Isle of Man.

Its construction extended over a long period and the earliest part is believed to date from 1153. However, the castle as we see it now dates from the 14th century. You enter the castle through the Barbican — the modestly-priced guidebook is recommended.

The site was known to have been used by the Norse kings to defend the fertile southern lowlands and, the castle's turbulent history saw it endure foreign raids and seige, as told in the *Historical Section*. ❏

Ramsey town trail

The port of Ramsey has a particularly fond place in Manx hearts, as it is the modern successor of the point at which the original Norse landings were made, including that of Godred Crovan, the King Orry of Manx legend

LIKE the other principal island towns, Ramsey grew up quite naturally around a natural harbour, in this case, the mouth of the Sulby River. The town dates from about the middle of the 17th century, when it would certainly have been very different from today.

Then, the river divided into two arms at its mouth, with one discharging into the sea in the vicinity of what is now the Mooragh Park and the other near the Old Cross. The older part of the town has now almost completely disappeared and has been replaced by the architecture of the 1960s. But, here and there, its old majesty survives, nowhere more so than in Parliament Street.

From the bus station, Parliament Street is a short walk down Christian Street, and then through the Victorian shopping precinct. It is truly a grand street which was started in its present form about 1800, and many buildings proudly bear testimony to their age with their date of completion incorporated in the façade. To my mind, it has retained its character and lost none of its charm with its wide variety of shops intermingled with banks, offices, public houses and — above all — houses in which people live.

Look at the façades above the shops where the date of building and, in some cases, the name of its original business, is often cast in stone. We head off to the right and make our way along the street as far as East Street and then on to the harbour.

Ahead of us is the swing bridge, to the left the shipyard, and to the right, the hustle and bustle of the commercial harbour which is still home to the trading coaster. The Stanley Hotel on the corner is one of the oldest pubs in the town and, as you walk past towards Market Place, look up now and again at the gables of the buildings and you will appreciate that Ramsey has always been very much an active port, with ship's chandlers and warehousing fronting the harbour. The frontages above today's shops and other premises give a hint of the past prosperity of the port area.

As we walked through Parliament Street you would, no doubt, have been intrigued by the numerous alleys leading to the harbour, so now is your chance to try one. We shall nip up the next one on the right just before the corner and here we are back in Parliament Street. The building opposite is the Courthouse and Police Station built around 1790 and designed by George Steuart, the architect who designed the Castle Mona in Douglas for the Duke of Atholl.

Bear round to the left until you enter Market Place, dominated by St Paul's Church, built in 1819 and consecrated in 1822 but much modified since. Behind it is the new development of St Paul's Square with more shops, all built on the site of Old Ramsey. Let's see if we can find any of it. As we walk down the seaward side of Market Place, look across at the front of what used to be the Saddle Hotel and admire the stucco work with all the saddles on the frontage. At the end of the Square look back at St Paul's,

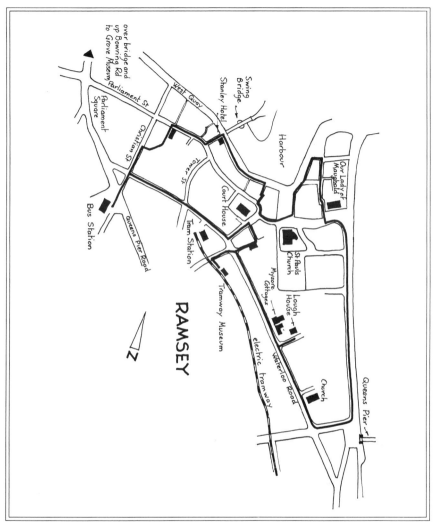

set against the magnificent backdrop of North Barrule. Continue along the Harbour to Neptune Street and into Mona Street, catching a glimpse of Old Ramsey before crashing into the 20th century as you walk out into Dale Street and onto the Promenade by the swimming pool.

We walk along the Promenade as far as the Queen's Pier, where you can see what remains of the old tramway (*see following*), then turn right up Queen's Drive and right again into Waterloo Road. A short distance towards the town centre we come across a little more of Ramsey's history at the Old Cross, which was the original market square at the side of the Sulby river where its southern arm joined the sea. The adjoining Lough House was built by Thomas Corlett, the Vicar General.

Continuing down Waterloo Road, we come next to the distinctive Mysore Cottages, built to the memory of Gen-

Although there has been much new development in Ramsey, the historic core remains — note St Paul's Church just beyond the bulk of the new buildings dominating the picture. The foreground shows the promenade, just north of Queen's Pier, while the swing bridge is clearly seen crossing the harbour (top right)

eral Sir Mark Cubbon who had been Commissioner General and Administrator of Mysore in India. Alongside these buildings is the distinctive shape of a school. This building, dating from 1864, was the Old Grammar School which was replaced in 1922 by the new school in Lezayre Road. A short distance further and we are at the junction with Parsonage Road.

Now you can visit the Electric Railway Museum next to the station and housed in the original running shed. There are a number of interesting exhibits, including the former Queen's Pier Tramway locomotive and train.

The Queen's Pier was built in 1886 and the tramway was 3ft gauge and originally provided a facility for hand-propelled luggage trucks. In 1937 a Planet petrol-engined locomotive and 15-seat trailer were acquired. In 1950 an 11-seat Wickham petrol engined railcar was added to the fleet. The tramway ceased operation in the mid 1970s.

Also to be seen are MER loco no.23, dating from 1900, and a bogie freight car which started life as a passenger car in 1895.

To glimpse a bit more of Old Ramsey, make a short detour down Chapel Lane, along College Street and into Peel Street, and back to Waterloo Road to make your way back to the bus station. On the way we pass the Albert Road schools which were built just after the turn of the century by the newly-formed School Board.

Before returning to Douglas and if you have not yet visited the Grove Rural Life Museum, which is based on a Victorian residence, why not take a No.20 bus which passes the door.

There are displays of toys, costumes, furniture and vehicles including period agricultural implements. The walk back to the town can be made via Mooragh Promenade and the park, while a little further north along the coast is an ancient earthwork. ❑

1. Groudle Glen Railway

TAKING IN ONCHAN AND PORT JACK

A two-mile (4km) walk. Allow one and a half to two hours. The main objective of this walk is the Groudle Glen Railway. The curious remains of a Victorian "zoo" are also seen, as is the historic heart of the village of Onchan

STARTING at the Derby Castle terminus of the Electric Railway, take the tram to Groudle. On alighting, look across at the Groudle Glen Hotel which still retains much of its original character from the time when it was the terminus of the Howstrake Estate Tramway.

We walk down through the Glen entrance and make for the terminus of the Groudle Glen Railway. This 2ft gauge line was originally built in 1896 to transport our Victorian forebears from the glen out along the headland to a terminus overlooking man-made pools which housed sea lions and polar bears. Today, the remains of this "zoo" have a rather spooky air and were used as a setting for the shoot-out in the episode of the *Lovejoy* TV series mentioned in *Section One*.

Two steam locomotives were provided by W G Bagnall Ltd of Stafford, both 2-4-0 tank engines named *Sea Lion* and *Polar Bear*, together with eight open carriages. Later, two battery-powered locomotives entered service, as well as a petrol-engined loco. After the second world war, *Sea Lion* was refurbished by cannibalising *Polar Bear* and the railway ran for some years before becoming derelict and abandoned in 1962. *Sea Lion* went off the island to a private museum.

It has recently returned, having been refurbished by apprentices from British Nuclear Fuels Ltd, at Sellafield, to operate on the now restored railway run by enthusiasts in the Isle of Man Steam Railway Supporters Association Ltd. It is worth checking the timetable as *Sea Lion* may be in steam — if so, a ride on this novel line should not be missed.

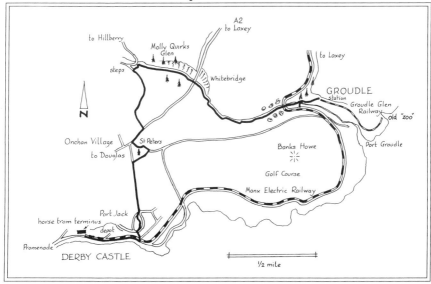

From the Groudle Glen Railway station, follow the path back to the river and take the path under the stone arches of the road bridge which also carries the tramway to Laxey. Pause to consider how the local contractor, Mark Carine, constructed these arches in 1894.

We follow the Groudle River to the Whitebridge, taking care when crossing the main Douglas to Laxey road, to continue following the river to the end of Molly Quirk's Glen. We must take the

The Groudle Glen Railway winds through lush vegetation

steps leading uphill out of the glen and follow School Road into the village of Onchan. Turn right at the main road and the next left towards St Peter's church. The area is known as the Butt and forms the nucleus of the Onchan Heritage Centre. This conservation area extends from the church to the main road. At its heart are some old cottages, one of which houses a collection of furniture and personal effects recalling the way of life when the cottages were built. The local heritage committee is enthusiastic and hopes, in time, to broaden the scope of the conservation area.

Captain Bligh, of Bounty fame, was married in Onchan parish church in 1781.

We shall walk through the churchyard, taking the pathway through the metal gate, onto Royal Avenue, turning left to Port Jack at the bottom of the road. Walk through the open glen to emerge above the tramway. The houses on both sides of the glen were requisitioned during the second world war and became the Onchan Internment Camp, originally housing 1,200 German intern-

ees. Towards the end of hostilities, the occupants were Italians.

Making our way down to the coast road, we pass a convenient fish and chip shop.

Continuing back towards Derby Castle, we pass the Manx Electric Railway depot which was built on the filled-in Port-e-Vada creek. The original power house can be seen at the back of the depot, with the repair shops, while to the right can be seen the running sheds. Back at Derby Castle, I would recommend a look around the Horse Tramway Museum, housed in the horse tram depot at Strathallan. It is certain to be open in the summer, and, if you are lucky, you might at least see the exhibits through an open door out of season.

What better way to end this short walk than with a ride along the promenade on a horse tram. Look for the Falcon Cliff incline railway as you approach the Palace Casino. The original was built in 1887 and was a twin track 4ft gauge operation, with two cars linking the Falcon Cliff Hotel to the Douglas Promenade. The railway was removed in 1896 and re-erected one year later at Port Soderick to link the resort to the terminus of the Marine Drive Tramway. The present 5ft gauge lift dates from 1927. ❏

Above — *the eerie remains of the zoo at Groudle Glen*

Right — *Laxey Wheel. See next walk*

Below — *Horse trams pass on Douglas Promenade*

2. Laxey Wheel

A one mile-plus (2 km) walk. Allow one and a half hours. A short walk around Laxey with the Mines Heritage trail as its objective

FROM the Manx Electric Railway leaving Douglas, let's go to South Cape. As we alight from the electric car (local people seldom refer to them as trams) we see the sign ahead of us announcing South Cape, for Old Laxey and the beach.

Leaving the stop, we follow the road down towards the sea at the junction with the Old Laxey Hill which is quickly reached. We turn right and walk up the hill for a short way, looking for a footpath sign pointing left down to the promenade.

Laxey beach is quite stony at high tide, but when the tide is out there is a pleasant stretch of sand, ideal for children. There are cafés and refreshment stalls too.

Making our way along the promenade to the harbour, we pass a large warehouse presently used in the manufacture of smoking pipes but built originally by the Great Laxey Mining Co, as indeed was the harbour. We continue to the area of the bridge and follow the bank of the river along a defined path until we come to the large factory-like building where we cross the river to join the Glen Road.

This is the point at which the major flooding occurred in 1930. The building opposite is the original Laxey Power Station, built in 1894 as one of three providing power for the Manx Electric Railway. It housed two Galloway boilers, providing steam for a pair of 90 hp engines driving two Mather Platt dynamos, producing 500 volts DC, at 100 Amps. The station was modified in 1903, with additional boilers and new triple expansion 400 hp steam engines to produce 7,000V AC at 25 cycles. It continued to operate until the flood. In 1934 the company ceased generating its own power and bought in electricity from the public supply.

We turn left over the bridge and continue up the Glen Road, passing the St George's Woollen Mills where you can see Manx tweed woven on hand looms. We continue straight on at the mills, beside the houses, into what was the area occupied by the washing floors of the Laxey Mines. Although much modified, some of the features can still be seen. Note particularly the series of ramps on the right, divided by walls — these are the remains of the old ore bunkers and what can be seen are the hoppers down which the ore was tipped from the main adit railway.

The 19-inch tramway ran underground for most of its length, bringing the ore in wagons from the mine shafts to the washing floors which were built in 1847. It is thought that the ore wagons were originally hauled by horse, steam locomotives being introduced in 1875. The arch under the viaduct through which ore trains entered the washing floors can also still be clearly seen.

After browsing around the washing floors, we shall cross the Laxey river near the road viaduct and make our way out onto the Captain's Hill which climbs from Lower Laxey, parallel to the washing floors. Our objective is the tram station at Laxey. We get there by walking up Captain's Hill for a short distance and up a few steps through a gap

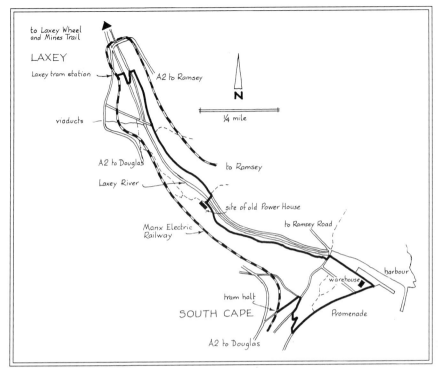

in the wall on the left.

The setting for Laxey station is superb and this is as good a way as any to see it for the first time — from the garden of a pub.

The Mines Tavern was originally the Mines Captain's house and it houses an interesting collection of photographs. An ideal lunch stop — even the bar looks like a tram.

Why not spend the afternoon in Laxey where you can inspect the Laxey Heritage Trust display adjoining the station before walking further up the valley towards the Laxey Wheel and the Laxey Mines Trail, which includes a short underground "experience". It is still being developed to embrace more of the extremely interesting industrial archaeology of the area.

Ore was hauled from the mine workings in a bucket-like device known as a "kibble" and discharged at adit level

into wagons to be taken to the washing floors for processing. The main adit provided the principal means of communication between the shafts and the washing floors. Rails were laid in the adit tunnel and it is believed that the ore wagons were hauled to the washing floors using horses.

Much research into the history of the mines is presently being undertaken and dates are being fixed more accurately. It can be said that betwen 1870 and 1875 access along the adit was improved and a 19-inch gauge railway was laid from the washing floors to serve the main shafts, with motive power being provided by two small steam locomotives. Their size was dictated by the tunnel height and they stood only 4ft 9 ins to the top of the chimney. The engines were 0-4-0 tank locomotives built by Lewin Engine Company, of Poole. They continued to work until the mine closed

Above — the crank on the giant Laxey Wheel connects to a rod which is carried along the graceful duct, below.

Below right — the view form the top of the wheel is spectacular, but not for the faint of heart

and were eventually scrapped in 1935.

The ore trains normally comprised seven wagons which were loaded directly over the shafts on a timber platform, while the locomotive negotiated the shaft head on a by-pass cut into the rock. The trains were assembled by hand shunting and then taken to the washing floors where the ore was discharged by gravity into storage bunkers.

Very few surface remains of the tramway can be seen but recent underground investigation has revealed the extent of the tramway, much of it intact. As more is learnt about the mine and its working, so the Mines Heritage Trail will become perhaps the most comprehensive of its type in the British Isles.

If you have had enough walking for today, you can take a ride to the top of Snaefell on the Snaefell Mountain Railway to view the island from its highest peak. There are superb views of the wheel and the Laxey valley, with the Snaefell Mines and the whole of the north of the island on the way up. If you are interested in the history of motorcycling on the island, you can break your journey at The Bungalow to visit the Motorcycle Museum. ❏

3. Cashtal yn Ard

From Glen Mona to Ballaglass

A three-mile (4.5km) walk. Allow one and a half hours. Can be muddy in places. The walk takes in a mixture of pre-historic and industrial archaeology

TAKE the Manx Electric Railway to Glen Mona (or, out of season, No.15, 15A or 15B bus). On the way, pay particular attention, after passing the dramatic cliff top journey round Bulgham Bay, to the Dhoon and the quarry on the right. This is Kion-e-Henin quarry which was operated by the former Highway Board. All of the buildings have now been removed, but stone was moved by aerial ropeway to a storage hopper above a siding specially built for the purpose in 1923.

Some rails can still be seen, and so too can the trackbed on top of the hedge. Within the quarry there was a 2ft gauge railway laid to take "Jubilee" trucks from the face to the crusher. There are no remains of this tramway but the ledge on which it ran can still be seen.

Dating from 1895 is the Dhoon granite quarry which lies on the other side of the main road. This was leased by the same directors as the Manx Electric Railway venture and sets were manufactured for the Douglas Cable Tramway, laying the foundations of a lucrative export venture. The quarry was connected to the Dhoon sidings by a narrow gauge tramway and stone was provided for other tramway purposes.

On arrival at Glen Mona, we follow the path down the glen to the ford on the Rhenab road, where we turn left and walk along the surfaced road for approximately half a mile. At a right angled bend in the road we must be careful to look for the signpost directing us to Cashtal-yn-Ard which we shall visit by means of a short path from the road.

Cashtal-yn-Ard displays the remains of a neolithic five-chambered tomb.

Returning to the road, we continue on our way downhill to Cornaa. As we start to see the houses of this little community we must be careful to look for a public right of way sign to Ballaglass, and turn left uphill on a narrow track which skirts Ballaglass Glen itself but affords a good view of some of the tallest trees to be found in the island. We continue on the track until it enters a field alongside the tramway. Be careful to follow the waymarkers and cross the track with care.

You will now see a very large building just below the track. This is the remains of the Ballaglass power station *(referred to in the description of the Manx Electric Railway in Section Two).* One of the large halls housed the engines and generators, and the other, a stand-by battery storage system. The buildings end-on to these were the boiler house and coal store. It all looks much the same from the outside as it did in 1898 except for a chimney made up from cast iron segments. Although now derelict, you can imagine the activity in its heyday, with two Robb-Armstrong tandem compound engines, driven by steam at a pressure of 120lbs per square inch and generating 240 Amps at 500V DC. There were separate generators for battery charging, the batteries being capable of providing full voltage at 140A for six hours.

Moving on, we follow the marked footpath to the Corrany and care is needed as the going can be a little muddy in places. On joining the main road, we turn right down the hill and continue over the bridge to look for a right of way sign leading off to the right to return to Ballaglass halt, from where the tram can be taken back to Douglas. (Out of season, catch the bus back from the main road.)

If we have time to spare we can take a walk through Ballaglass Glen, admiring the natural gorge formed by the Cornaa River, with its numerous waterfalls and the 17 acres of varied woodland. In the glen, you will come across the wheelcase and office buildings of the Great Mona Mining Company. The workings were started in 1854, with levels at 60ft and 144ft, and yielded at least some lead ore. The Great Mona Company recommenced mining in 1866 and reached a depth of 300ft (91m). By 1868 the work was abandoned and the mine closed. ❑

Cashtal yn Ard, looking north towards North Barrule

58

4. Maughold Church

BALLAJORA, PORT MOOAR AND PORT E VULLEN

A three-mile (6.5km) walk. Allow two and a half hours. The natural rugged beauty of this cliff walk takes in some of the sites of the haematite (iron ore) mining in the island, as well as Maughold church yard with its Celtic crosses.

TAKE the Manx Electric Railway from Derby Castle to Ballajora halt from where we walk downhill to Port Mooar, admiring the view over Maughold.

Turning off the Ballajora road, we follow the coastal path signs to arrive on the stony foreshore of Port Mooar. You may notice the unusual bamboo type grass growing beside the road and there is more on the path around the headland. It would be interesting to know how it got there — perhaps from the wreck of a vessel carrying grain or seed?

However, we make off to the left, following the signs, to walk around the headland of Gob ny Portmooar (headland of the great harbour). If we are lucky, we may see common seals basking on the rocks.

Notice the ruddy colour of the earth and the rocks adjoining the path and you will have a clue to the fact that haematite (iron ore) was mined in this area. Rounding the headland, Maughold Head lighthouse comes into view, along with three distinct beaches below the cliffs which clearly show the rock strata. The nearest is Dhyrnane, where a mine was opened in 1857. A shaft was sunk to a depth of 420ft and two levels were driven. Although a considerable quantity of haematite was obtained, its presence was sporadic and the mine appears to have ceased working by the end of the 19th century.

We climb up the path from the coast, going over a stile to walk through a field before joining a grassy track leading through Baldromma Mooar farm, to join the Maughold Head lighthouse road by a gate which gives access to the churchyard. A short distance before reaching this point, we passed a fine example of a lime kiln, typical of many in various parts of the island.

A detour into the churchyard is worth the effort as there is a good selection of Celtic stone crosses dating from the mid seventh century. These are housed in a covered display, while opposite stands the 14th century Maughold Pillar Cross.

Returning to the road, we follow the coastal path signs to Maughold Head and turn on to Manx National Trust land. If we pause and look back over the village, there is a good view of North Barrule, while to the right of the village, the Glebe mine had minor workings which produced haematite in small quantities.

We follow the well signposted path over Maughold Head. Below us, at Cor Stack (round stack, as applied to a rock sitting in isolation) we may again see seals basking. As the path starts to drop towards the cliff edge, we see the predominant shape of Stack Mooar (the big stack). We continue along a level path through disused workings, originally connected with haematite production from Maughold Head Mines, although later used to win building stone.

A little further on, we can see the remains of surface workings and the shaft collar of the mine at Gob Ago. The mines at one time employed 70 men and shipped ore regularly to Whitehaven. Ahead of us is the grand view over

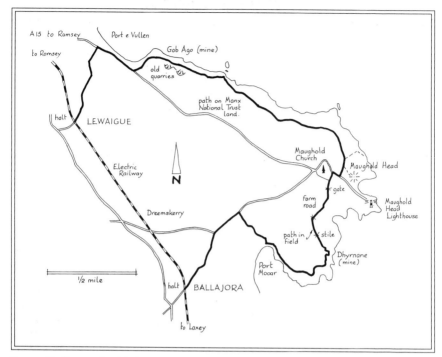

Port-e-Vullen and Tableland Point, with Ramsey Bay and the Bride Hills stretching out into the distance, and the Point of Ayre beyond. To our left is Slieau Lewaigue, with North Barrule dominant in the background. The path takes us back to the main road. Here we turn right and walk a short distance to the bottom of the hill, to turn left by the disused chapel and up Jack's Lane to Lewaigue Halt, where we catch the tram back to Douglas.

Morning is the best time for this walk and if you have spent the morning enjoying its splendour, why not spend the afternoon in Ramsey? *See Ramsey Town Trail, page 48.* ❏

5. Marine Drive

FROM PORT SODERICK TO DOUGLAS

A 3¹/₂ (6km) walk. Allow two hours. An easy coastal ramble along the route of the former Douglas Head Marine Drive and Electric Tramway

WE TAKE the steam railway to Port Soderick. The alternative No.29 bus runs only in the afternoon in winter, so starting the walk in the morning means walking an extra two miles along the Old Castletown Road to Port Soderick.

From the station, walk downhill, under the embankment and take the path on the right down through the trees. Just before the bridge at the bottom of the hill be careful to take the path into the glen, following the Crogga river which should be on your right. The glen opens out into a flat grassy area which is a sun-trap in the height of summer.

We soon come out of the glen at Port Soderick, which is only a shadow of its former self. It was once a glorious Victorian watering place and pleasure boats sailed from Douglas to land at the jetty. There were many attractions and entertainments, and the present buildings provided summer shows and dancing until the late 1970s.

We walk along the promenade and look for right of way signs directing us up a flight of steps. These follow the line of the funicular cliff lift which connected the Port Soderick terminus of the Douglas Southern Electric Tramways Ltd to the entertainments below.

This was originally the Falcon Cliff incline railway, built in 1887 as a twin track 4ft gauge line, with two cars linking the Falcon Cliff Hotel to the Douglas Promenade. It was removed to Port Soderick in 1897. As we climb the steps, we can make out some of the supports to the funicular even now, although it is all very overgrown.

From the top of the steps we quickly join the Marine Drive, south of Keristal. This section of roadway is not part of the original Marine Drive which ran inland from Keristal to Oakhill. At Keristal, the road swings across the head of the glen to continue north on the alignment of the original road and tramway. If we look up on the left we can just see some rusting metal fence posts made from the old steel sleepers of the tramway, which was lifted in stages between 1955 and 1960. The Marine Drive came into Manx Government ownership in 1946 and a scheme was promoted to build a modern road along the coast. But it was 1963 before it was completed.

Since then, it has suffered from rock falls and the erosion of some filled areas, which has resulted in its closure to vehicles for the present. It remains open to pedestrians and we can walk through the gate to carry on our way.

As we round the first real corner at Rhebog (from the Scandinavian Ripirk, meaning rocky creek), look over the stone wall down to the beach and you will see the remains of a Dutch coaster, *MV Grietje*, which ran aground here in a snowstorm in 1963, the crew having to be rescued by breeches buoy by the Douglas cliff rescue brigade.

The next spectacular section is the Whing, where the contorted rock strata found on this part of the east coast are vividly displayed. As we round the next corner, the features of the drive become softer and the original trackbed of the tramway can almost be seen. The headland on our right is Little Ness and this

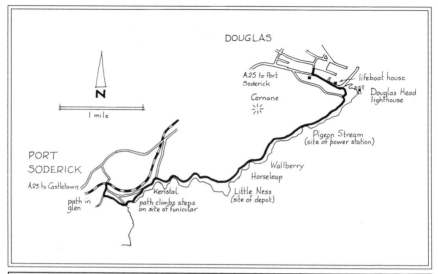

The southern part of Marine Drive, looking north

was the site chosen for the tram depot, as it was the only area of land within the ownership of the company that was flat enough. You can see the area occupied by the car shed just below the road and if you look in the shrubbery you can see where the inspection pits were.

The gap in the fence is where the spur joined the four-track depot to the main tramway line. The depot was originally

The Marine Drive toll gate — trams ran through the left hand arch and carriages through the right. There were ornamental gates and a house on the right in which the tollkeeper lived

served by a traverser, later converted to pointwork subsequently removed to the National Tramway Museum at Crich, Derbyshire, where preserved car No.1 can be seen, still in working order.

The drive is full of surprises and none greater than the one we get as we round the next corner to open up the view of the gully at Horseleap. The modern road was blasted into the rock face, but the original tramway crossed the gully on a wooden trestle bridge, replaced in 1896 by a single span steel bridge of 120ft (36.5m) on a gradient of 1 in 60. The original stone buttresses can still clearly be seen.

In 1978 the fill on the seaward side of the roadway was undermined by the action of the sea and the resulting slip caused the road to be closed to traffic. We walk round the slip on the rockbed cut out of the cliff, to be confronted by the second gully at which major engineering works were carried out by the tram company.

Again, the company built a two-span timber bridge to cross Wallberry, in 1893, and this too was replaced by a lattice two-span bridge in 1896, and the total span was 253ft (78m) and here, too, the original buttresses and the centre pier can be seen from the new road alignment. It certainly must have been an exhilarating experience travelling on the open top deck of the tramcar to spring off the edge of the cliff and cross the gap at Wallberry.

As we round the corner after Wallberry, the Drive meanders its way downhill towards the toll gate house, the top of which can just be seen in the distance. Before we reach it, we cross an embankment near a small car park. This is Pigeon Stream and the site of the power generating equipment.

The boiler room, which housed two horizontal water tube boilers, was at the present car park level. The two Browett-Lindley horizontal steam engines and generator sets were in the next floor down and, below that, was a pump room with condensers, feed pumps and cooling water pumps. The site was chosen because of the ready supply of water from the stream. The third major civil engineering structure crossed the inlet on the site of the present embankment and its total length was 114ft (35m). The original bridge is buried under the embankment and most of the fill material came from the power house.

Next we see the remains of the toll gate — its ornamental arches are all that remain. The trams passed through the landward arch, horse-drawn carriages through the other, and pedestrians through the turnstile. That is the way we go.

As we round the corner, leaving the Drive, the grand view of Douglas Bay opens before us. Get the map out and identify the hills ahead — Greeba is on the left, Snaefell is easily distinguished, with its aerial masts, and, on the right, is Banks Howe.

We must be careful to go down the steps by the bus turning area. We are walking beside the trackbed of the Douglas Head Incline Railway which connected the tramway and the Battery Pier. It was a double-track funicular with two cars built by Hurst Nelson and Co, the cable being operated by an oil engine at the head of the incline. It was demolished in the mid-1950s.

We also pass a real rarity on our right, sadly in a deteriorating state, the Great Union Camera Obscura. Our path goes left here between two walls which carried the funicular track over the path. As we descend the steps, the position of the railway is clearly seen alongside.

We can also see the old breakwater, built in 1879, and the new, extended one, completed in 1982, which protects Douglas harbour from south-east and easterly gales. We also pass the futuristic gas storage tank which contrasts dramatically with the camera obscura.

We continue along the harbour approach road and come across the life-boat house. The present boat, the RNLB *Sir William Hillary*, came on station in 1989 and is named after the founder of the Royal National Lifeboat Institution who lived at nearby Fort Anne. If the boathouse is open, it is well worth paying a visit, as there is a good selection of photographs and the service record boards make very interesting reading. The boat is one of the latest 47ft Tyne class and the cost of providing the service is met entirely by voluntary contribution.

Sir William Hillary arrived to settle in the Isle of Man a bankrupt, having lost a fortune raising an army to fight for king and country against France. The organisation he founded was originally called The National Institution for the Preservation of Life from Shipwreck.

We are almost back in Douglas now — cross the swing bridge to reach the the bus station. Although the present bridge is a replacement for the original one built in 1895, the accumulator and hydraulic rams which operate it are original and housed in the buildings on our left. ❏

6. The Silverburn

FROM BALLASALLA AND RUSHEN ABBEY

A three-mile (5km) walk. Allow two hours. A ramble mostly in woodland embracing a mixture of religious history and industrial archaeology

Rushen Abbey, with the abbey church in the background

THIS walk is centred on Ballasalla and the recently introduced Silverburn Experience, where a number of rights of way have been incorporated into walks of varying lengths, all adjoining the Silverburn River, between Ballasalla and Castletown. A leaflet is available from Tourist Information Centres, which describes the walks which vary in length from one to three miles (1.5-6km).

We are going to do our own exploration of the Silverburn and, to start, we must catch the train to Ballasalla (bus No.1, 1A or 8 in winter) and walk through the village to Rushen Abbey, walking down Mill Road at the rear of the Abbey Church. Crossing the Silverburn River, we can, if we wish, visit the grounds of the Abbey, now a tourist attraction with an historical garden, visitor centre, tea room and parts of the ruined remains of the original abbey.

The abbey was built by the monks of Furness Abbey, near Barrow, following a gift of land in 1134 by Olaf I, the youngest son of Godred Crovan and King of Mann between 1113 and 1153. Although originally a Benedictine order, the monks of Rushen Abbey adopted the Cistercian principles, becoming active farmers and a dominant influence in the island. The abbey was the last to be suppressed under the Reformation, being dissolved in 1540. The abbey tower, parts of the Sacristy and the Guest House remain.

Two Viking Kings of Mann were buried at Rushen Abbey, Reginald II in 1250 and Magnus, the last Norse king, in 1265. By far the most important legacy from the monks of Rushen Abbey is the *Chronicon Manniae* (the Chronicles of Mann) which form the earliest written record of events in the island.

From the abbey, we continue alongside the west wall till we almost join the main road, taking the public footpath

through the farmland at Ballahot, with the lime quarries of Billown to our left, where some of the oldest quarries and kilns in the island can still be seen.

On joining the main road, walk a short distance before turning left along the road to Grenaby which we follow for a mile, with South Barrule ahead of us. On the summit, you can make out the rim of the rampart of the hill fort which contained a considerable number of huts dating from 523BC.

As we drop down into Grenaby, we must be careful not to miss the path on our right which will take us back along a most beautiful part of the Silverburn

River to Athol Bridge, where we again cross the main road to continue along the Silverburn River. As we approach Silverdale, we come across a boating lake and children's playground with a café which makes a pleasant place to stop for refreshments.

The boating lake belies the earlier history of the old building adjoining the café. The building is the Creg Mill which was one of two mills originally built by the monks of Rushen Abbey. The boating lake was originally the dammed mill pond, providing water for the wheel which still turns. The roundabout is worth more than a passing glance as it

The ancient Monks' Bridge across the Silverburn

too is water-powered, by a wheel which was originally in use at the Foxdale mines.

Suitably refreshed, we continue downstream, following the waymarkers and passing the site of the Ballasalla Ochre and Umber Works, now converted to a private residence. The company was a sizeable one, with warehousing in Castletown, from which exports were made, and the north quay at Castletown still carries the name Umber Quay — a reminder of the past activity.

Continuing, we shortly come across the Crossag Bridge or Monks' Bridge. Almost certainly the oldest surviving crossing of the river, this packhorse bridge was built by the monks of Rushen Abbey and dates from the 14th century. We are almost back at the abbey itself and, as we cross the bridge to return to the village, we pass the Abbey Mill. Now converted to residential use, it was attached to the abbey and was a substantial mill with an internal wheel. We

The gardens at Rushen Abbey — now ideal for a picnic or a quiet wander

shall wander back through the village to return to Douglas by train. ❑

7. St Michael's Isle

CASTLETOWN TO DERBYHAVEN AND DERBY FORT

A three and a half-mile (6km) walk on level ground to visit historic and religious relics. Allow two hours

TAKING the train (No. 1, 1A or 8 bus in winter) we travel to Castletown and the object is to visit the castle. The bus will drop you outside the castle but from the railway station there is a short walk along the harbour.

Leaving the station, we turn left and walk to the Castletown promenade, towards Derbyhaven, passing Hango Hill *(see Manx Meander, Stage 8)*, turning right at Derbyhaven to walk out onto the peninsula of Langness, bearing left and continuing around the sweep of Derbyhaven bay. The area is always interesting, with many small craft anchored in the protected water. Oyster-catchers abound, foraging on the edge of the tide. At low water you will often see a heron stealthily awaiting his moment to strike. We walk past the Castletown Golf Links Hotel over the causeway to St Michael's Isle.

To our right is the distinctive outline of the chapel of St Michael, dating from the 12th century, and believed to be built on the site of an earlier Celtic keeill. Ahead of us is the Derby Fort, thought to have been built originally by Edward Stanley, the third Early of Derby, during the 16th century. The fort was repaired and strengthened to take a full culverin (heavy cannon) and other armament to defend the island from invasion by Cromwell. The work was carried out under the direction of James, the seventh Earl of Derby.

We retrace our steps to the ruined farm, where we cross to the other shore of the peninsula to walk around the edge of Sandwick Bay. Sandvik is another Scandinavian word, meaning sandy creek. The area along which we are walking adjoining the golf course is the site of the Derby horse races which were introduced by the "Great Earl" and reintroduced by his son, Charles, the eighth Earl of Derby, after the Restoration.

We join the road again near Hango Hill but only stay on it a short while, before walking back to Castletown through the grounds of King William's College, founded in 1668 by Bishop Barrow. The present buildings, designed by the architect John Welch and completed in 1833, were rebuilt after a disastrous fire in 1844.

Turning left on the main road, it is only a short walk back into the town to visit the castle and take refreshment before returning to Douglas.

See also Castletown Town Trail, page 45.

❏

Derby Fort on a grey winter's day

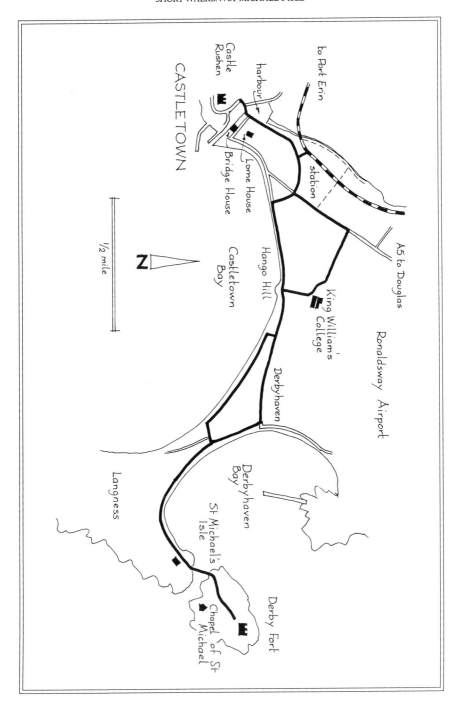

8. Cregneash

A two-mile (4km) walk, to visit the folk museum at Cregneash. Allow two and a half hours. Although this walk is a short one, it is fairly strenuous

WE TAKE the steam train from Douglas to Port Erin (No.1, 1A or 8 bus in winter). Leaving the station, we turn left into Station Road and pass the Steam Railway Museum which we must visit later. We turn left and follow Strand Road to the Promenade — the view across Port Erin Bay is superb.

Bradda Head, surmounted by Milner's Tower is to our right, and the headland of Kione-ny-Garee (meaning the end of the thicket) is on the left, while running across the bay behind the Albert Pier are the remains of the breakwater which was destroyed in 1884 and which is mentioned in *Stage 7 of the Manx Meander.*

We walk along the promenade past the recently renovated Bay Hotel, and up the steep track alongside the building to emerge at the Darrag. We turn left along the unmade road until we reach the end of the row of houses, turning right up Ballnahowe Road.

Cregneash is very much a working museum

We soon come onto the open moorland of the Mull Hill (or Meayl Hill, meaning bald or bare hill) and to the left of the road you can see a fenced area almost on top of the hill. We follow the path from the road to the Meayl Circle, a Megalithic monument containing a number of Neolithic burial chambers, which is described and pictured in the *Historic Section* at the start of the book *(page 8).*

We walk to the top of the hill, passing the remains of the second world war look-out posts, and follow the rough road to Cregneash village which we can see below us, its thatched cottages contrasting with the Civil Aviation Authority navigation beacon on the hilltop opposite. Ahead of us is a view over the Calf of Man and we can get some idea of its size from here. On a clear day you may be able to see the Irish Mourne Mountains in the distance.

Cregneash (derived from the Scandinavian Krakuness, meaning crow ness, the old name of the promontory forming Spanish Head and Black Head) is now preserved as a typical upland crofting village and is largely owned by the Manx National Trust and the Trustees of the Manx Museum who maintain a number of the buildings as a folk museum. The farm is run on traditional lines and a short walk around the village and farm will give us an insight into a past way of life, before we make our way back to Port Erin. You can even hear the taped words of Harry Kelly, the last person to speak Manx as his first language, and see Manx Loaghtan sheep.

As we leave the village and join the Sound Road, we turn right to pass Cregneash Quarry. The view ahead is north along the length of the island, with Port St Mary in the foreground, the sweep of Bay ny Carricky and Langness peninsula in the right distance, with the central hills forming the backdrop.

We have to be careful not to get carried away with the view as we have to take the right of way to the left, by the mountain wall skirting the Mull Hill. There are a number of ways down off the hill, but I suggest we walk almost to the road before turning down the "Golden Road", to the right through Ballnahowe, on a reasonable track which eventually peters out in a field at Ballnahowe. If we are careful, we can pick up the waymarkers but if in doubt carry on down,

crossing over the hedge before reaching the houses. We appear to be in a private drive but don't worry — the right of way was there before the house. We turn right and walk down Baymount, left onto St Mary's Road, and right at Ballafurt Road and we are back where we started.

Buses and trains both leave the village from the railway station in Station Road. ❑

Traditional Manx cottages at Cregneash — the design is similar to those found in other Celtic countries, principally Ireland and the Hebrides

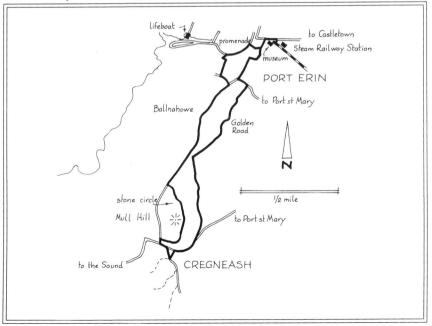

71

9. Foxdale mines

A WALK ROUND THE "BACK OF THE MOON"

*A seven and a half-mile (12km) walk.
Allow four hours. The walk touches on a
number of industrial archaeological remains of the Foxdale mining activity and
finishes at historic St John's*

TAKE the No.5 or 6 bus from Douglas as far as Crosby, getting off at the Post Office.

Walk down Station Road, and, passing the playing fields on our right, we come to the site of the former Crosby railway station. Turn right, and follow the signs indicating the Railway Heritage Trail. Pause and imagine the former activity at this station with its cattle dock and goods shed. Even in the last years of operation, trains were scheduled to pass at this station.

We shall head off in a westerly direction along the former track, passing the main engineering works depot of the Manx Government, on the left, built on the site of an old quarry which earlier provided stone for highway construction. The former railway track ran through the central valley from Douglas to Peel, and the section on which we are walking was built on extremely boggy land, or Curragh, and as we walk under the stony outcrop of Creg y Whallian, having passed Cooilingel crossing, we can really see the natural vegetation of the Curragh.

The hill which we see on our right is Greeba (the peak 1,375ft (423m), with Slieau Roy further to the right. The next road crossing is at the Ballacurry road, and here we turn left and walk through the farmyard and up the surfaced road between two high hedges. As we come out from between these hedges, we find

Ghost of the past — Cornelly mines with Greeba in the background

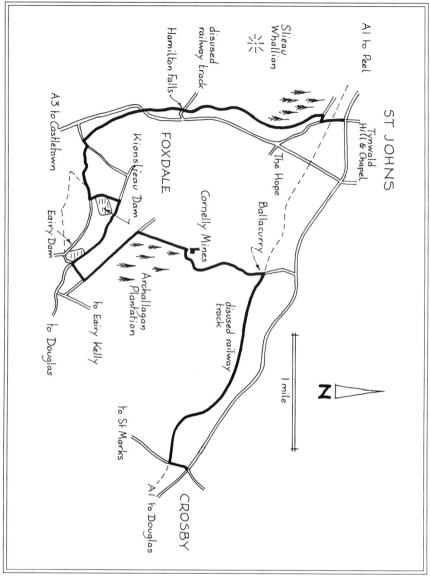

ourselves on a slight plateau overlooking Greeba mountain and looking east down the central valley. This is certainly one of the best views of Greeba you can find. Can you see the outline of Greeba Castle in the trees? It was the one-time residence of Hall Caine, the celebrated Manx author.

Having had our breather, we now start to climb in earnest, being careful to take a sharp right turn and continue up between the overgrown hedges either side of what has now become a very rough stony track. At the top of the hill, the view opens out and to our right, ahead of us, is the Townsend or Cor-

This pre-war scene at Foxdale station shows IMR loco No.8, Fenella, which was undergoing restoration at the time of publication. The spoil heaps on the right help to illustrate how the area became known as the Back of the Moon

nelly Mines where we will stop and look at the surface remains.

The mine was worked prior to 1845, but the present buildings date from 1878 and operations stopped in 1886. There were two shafts dug 36ft (22m) apart. Engine shaft was the deepest, at 140 fathoms. A high quality galena (lead ore) was found together with some semi-precious crystal.

There was an earlier working, known as the Mountain shaft, some distance east of the present remains, which was abandoned when the new shafts were sunk.

The largest structure comprises the remains of the engine house at the head of the New Engine Shaft which connected at 80 fathoms to the Engine Shaft.

Leaving the mines, we walk uphill on the surfaced road, passing Cornelly House and Archallagan Plantation on our left. Looking to our right we can see the outline of the peaks of Slieau Whallian and our walk will take us back to St John's under the flank of the hill. At the

junction at the top of the hill, we turn left, skirting the plantation, and after about half a mile (1km), just before reaching Manx Radio's transmission masts, we turn right through the trees down a waymarked path.

At the bottom of the path we reach the Eairy and turn right, taking care to walk straight ahead at the next corner, following the Lhoobs Road with the Eairy Dam on our left. It is always worth stopping at any time of the year to see what birdlife is on the water. Ducks and geese are always there, and we may see the occasional heron and swans, besides the inevitable gulls. Migrant birds can be seen, too, and in winter, when the dam is frozen, swans and geese become confused and land in a sliding flurry of wings and feathers before coming to a bemused stop.

The dam was built to provide water for the Far Gin mine (later to become the Central Foxdale mine) and the associated sawmill. Workings started in the early 1820s but came to a halt by 1860.

The workings were re-opened in 1871 and work was concentrated on three shafts — Elizabeth, Amy and Taylor's — which reached depths of 145, 40 and 74 fathoms respectively. The mine was productive and the lead ore had a high silver content.

Continuing along the road, we see a second dam which was also built to provide water for the numerous water wheels at the Foxdale mines, and our walk will take us across the head of the dam. We turn left off the road and walk through the edge of a plantation to emerge briefly in the open, overlooking the water of the Kion Slieau dam. We join the road and turn right to walk towards

The old Foxdale line is now a pleasant walk

Foxdale village. On our left are the surface remains of the spoil heaps and washing floors associated with Potts shaft. Note the clock tower on the corner as we come into the village.

We carry on into the bottom of the valley by the former playing fields (now a primary school) and, although the works on the left are used for sand and gravel processing, the buildings are based on the original ones associated with the Foxdale mines and their washing floors. Behind them are the remains of Beckwiths Shaft winding house, now converted to a workshop, and on the hill to the left is Bawdens Shaft. On our right, now brightly painted, is the old railway station building.

We are going to walk down the old track of the Foxdale Railway to St John's. Before we start, look at the road opposite the station and see if you can see the remains of the railway crossing that connected the railway yard to the mines yard — it is the only piece of track that is still in place.

Local people here used to refer to the siding leading from the back of the railway station to the mine as *The Back of the Moon* when the mines were still working, and hence the sub-title to this walk. The area was even more like a moonscape by the 1950s, but the spoil heaps and dereliction are now gone.

The railway is now a right of way and we walk behind the miners' cottages on our left. We soon come to the location of the former Luke's Bridge where the railway used to cross the road on a splay. The bridge was removed and the road realigned when the track was removed in 1975. The railway approached this bridge on a high stone embankment, the remains of which can still be seen.

Follow the waymarkers to regain the track on the other side of the road, and we soon come to the site of Waterfall Halt, the only intermediate station on this branch. The station served Lower Foxdale and gave access to Hamilton Falls, a series of waterfalls much admired by the Victorians, now only partly seen from the main road.

We continue downhill under Slieau Whallian and emerge on a ledge overlooking Greeba and part of the Central Valley. The railway would have presented a spectacular sight with trains working hard up the 1 in 49 gradient against the backdrop of Slieau Whallian. The path soon disappears into a cutting and skirts the plantation and is unfortunately wet underfoot. We must be careful as we come out of the plantation to walk away from the trackbed to the left to join the road. The reason is that the railway crossed the river on two spans of a high girder bridge and the spans are no longer there, although the abutments and the central pier are still visible.

We are soon at St John's and, following the signpost directions to Tynwald Hill, we find ourselves in Station Road. The ceremonial hill is clearly visible ahead of us.

As we pass the pub and the Central Mart look on the right at the open space. It is hard to believe that this was the site of St John's station which was described earlier as the island's "Crewe Junction".

Two lines crossed the road on a level crossing, one bound for Peel and the other, nearest to the hill, for Ramsey. There were two platforms, with four tracks, a number of sidings and a signal box and, behind that, a large carriage shed. Despite all this, the station building was only a very simple timber-built structure with an office and a waiting room. On a typical Tynwald Day, even as late as the mid 1960s, St John's station was a bustling hive of activity.

As we get closer to the Hill, we pass the much more elaborate stone-built St John's station for the Foxdale line, now used as a private residence, and you can just make out the line of the trackbed where it crossed under the road and curved off towards Foxdale.

We join the main Douglas to Peel road opposite Tynwald Hill and it is from here that we shall catch our bus back to Douglas. We will first have a look at the Hill which is a four-tiered assembly place based on the Norse Thingvollr (Parliament Field) where the annual midsummer parliament has been held on July 5 since the period of the Norse Kingdom of Man, and is still held to this day. Here, Manx citizens enjoy the right to petition Parliament directly at a ceremony at which the laws passed by the members of the House of Keys are proclaimed in both English and Manx. July 5 is a national holiday in the Isle of Man and there is a big fair adjacent to the Hill each year.

We can walk along the processional way to St John's Church — which is strewn with reeds on Tynwald Day — and, in the field behind the Church, look at the Millennium Stone which was erected to celebrate 1,000 years of Government in the island in 1979.

There are descriptive plaques which give a brief account of the proceedings of Tynwald but if you are really interested in finding out more about the island's unique form of Government, you must visit the National Museum in Douglas. *See also the first, historical, section of this book.*

Also worth a visit is the Manx National Park — an attractive arboretum planted in 1979. ❏

Manx people enjoy a right of petition at Tynwald — these women are protesting about the pollution of the Irish Sea by the Sellafield nuclear plant. They are wearing traditional sprigs of Bollan bane (St John's wort)

Manxman's Meander

HAVING whetted their appetites on the shorter walks in the previous section, readers may now be ready for some of the Isle of Man's bigger challenges. The first part of this section of the book we have called A Manxman's Meander, or Manx Meander for short. It comprises a series of coast and fell walks, each distinct in its own right, and offering the possibility of returning to a base in Douglas on completion. However, the walks can be linked together to form a superb route, taking in the best of the Manx highlands and the wildest coast, which can be completed in seven or eight days.

The second part of this section features other recognised long-distance routes on the island, some having their origin in the 1979 celebrations of the Isle of Man government's millennium.

Each department of government was asked to participate in the celebrations marking 1,000 years of parliament and, for the highway authority, this was a somewhat difficult task, dealing as it normally does, with the mundane.

What eventually transpired was the introduction of the island's first long-distance footpath which was named *The Millennium Way*. It was based on the ancient ridgeway used by the Norse kings from their ancient landing place at Skyhill, to travel to their fortress on the southern plains. This became Castle Rushen, as recorded in the Chronicle of Man and the Isles (the *Chronicon Manniae et Insularum* of the monks of Rushen Abbey).

Two other long distance paths were introduced in Heritage Year, 1986. The longest was a coastal path, and the shorter one was based on the old herring road between Peel and the ancient capital, Castletown. Meetings between the Manx Heritage Foundation and the highway authority resulted in the two paths being named *Raad ny Foillan* (meaning road of the gull) and *Bayr ny Skeddan* (meaning the herring road).

After the amalgamation of a number of former administrative departments of government, following the introduction of a ministerial system of government in 1986, the Department of Highways, Ports and Properties has been able to add a further long distance path based on the former railway track between Douglas and Peel which has been developed as the *Railway Heritage Trail*.

All these longer routes are shown on the map, overleaf. It is recommended that, in addition to the sketch maps in this book, walkers should also carry either sheet 95 of the Ordnance Survey's 1:50,000 series, or — better still — the Isle of Man Highway and Transport Board's 1:25,000 map of public rights of way. A compass is also a wise safeguard on the hill sections. ❑

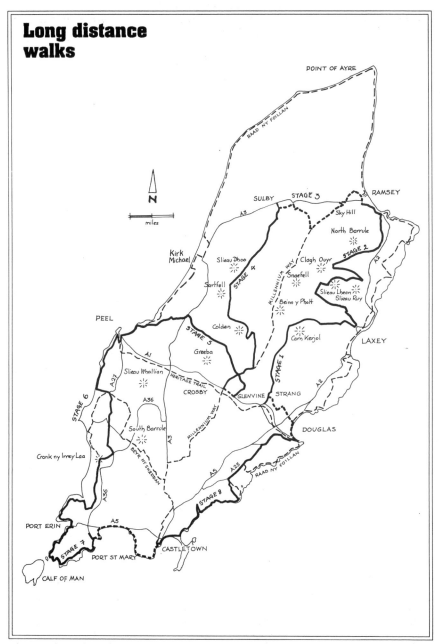

The map shows the eight stages of the Manxman's Meander (bold lines) and, in light hatched lines, the four other "official" long-distance routes where they differ from the Meander. The bold hatched lines represent the optional link sections of the Meander for those combining the stages into a week's walking

Douglas/Strang to Laxey

*An eight-mile (13km) walk with the option of
starting at The Strang or Douglas. The latter
option adds three miles (5km). Allow four or
five hours in total. Eating facilities and
accommodation in Laxey, where the famous
wheel and Mines Trail should be visited*

THE first stage of the Manx Meander starts at the Strang, near Douglas — a short bus trip from the capital on the No.5, 9 or 9A. For those preferring to go on foot, directions are given after those for the walk proper.

From the crossroads at the Strang, take the East Baldwin road past the Strang Stores. On the right you will see a water tower which was originally built in 1867 to serve the lunatic asylum. The building now forms the central point of the mental hospital.

After a short distance walking on the roadway, a view of the central hills opens up, with Greeba (a Scandinavian word meaning "peak") and Slieau Roy (Red Mountain) on the left, and Slieau Ree and, beyond it, Karn Kerjol, more correctly Slieau Chiarn Gerjoil (meaning the cairn of the devil), on the right. The central hills will be described in more detail later, but this is a good place to stop, look at the map and identify the hills by name. We shall head for the saddle between Karn Kerjol and Mullagh Ouyr (dun summit) and the hut on the skyline is a good landmark.

Head downhill at the junction to East Baldwin to cross Sir George's bridge, named after Sir George Drinkwater, a former mayor of Liverpool, who contributed to the cost of building the original bridge. On our right is a flat area alongside the River Glass (white stream). This was the site of the locomotive shed

and a depot with four sidings which formed part of the West Baldwin Reservoir Tramway. We passed one of the quarries used in the construction of the dam just before the bridge. The clay pit for the dam was at Ballacreetch, slightly to our right and on higher ground. To reach it the tramway used a reversing switchback, or zig-zag, and we shall walk beside part of its route, although there are no visible remains left.

A little further on we cross a second bridge and turn sharp left, following the footpath sign to Abbeylands and then the track between the hedges. It can be wet and muddy at any time of year.

Emerging at the top of this path, we turn left on the road and follow it for a short distance until we reach Abbeylands Chapel where we turn left again up a narrower, surfaced roadway.

This road is one of a number of ancient highways in the island, some remnants of which are surfaced and in constant use, while the remainder are the domain of walkers and others engaged in outdoor pursuits. Don't be surprised to encounter motorcyclists on these tracks — this is the Isle of Man and, of course, they have every right to be there. However, on this particular road you are more likely to encounter riders on horseback, it being a popular trek with nearby stables.

As we pass the farm buildings at Ballamenagh, be careful to follow the

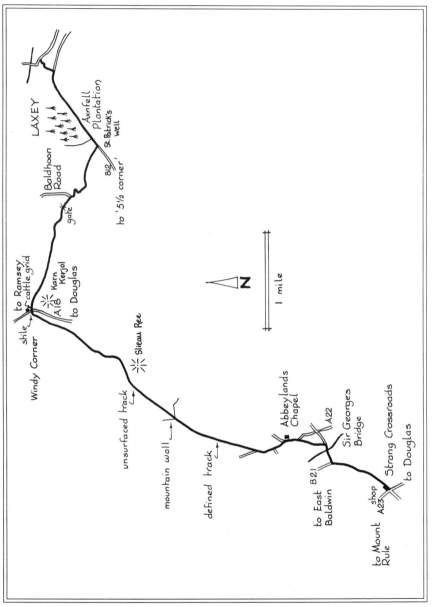

road slightly right and then straight on, ignoring the road to the left. The road quickly degenerates into an unsurfaced track with a predominantly white stone appearance and starts to climb up the southern slopes of Slieau Ree. The Manx Gaelic name of this mountain is a little obscure as the Manx language was largely a spoken one and several meanings with the same sound give the hill the name of "King's mountain" or "Red Mountain".

As we come to the top of the defined track, the shape of the hill ahead is quite clear and I prefer to think of the hill as the Red Mountain — in autumn it is a rich purple and, in winter, a deep rusty red. Pause a while and look behind you and you can see Douglas and the harbour and an expanse of the south of the island, with South Barrule dominating the view to the right.

Cross the stile and enter the "mountain land". The line of the old road is easily followed. It can be a little wet, even in summer, and the going, although on a gentle gradient, is heavy over heather and ling. Skirt the hill and you will see the Snaefell mountain road above and ahead of you. The old road follows the curve of Slieau Ree and crosses a minor landslip where care is needed to avoid losing the line of the track. It then follows the Snaefell mountain road and, although never more than 100 yards away, the hustle and bustle of traffic passing the 33rd milestone on the famous TT course can not be seen or heard. As we walk through a small rock cutting we almost expect to meet a horse and cart coming towards us with its load of peat heading for Douglas.

As we come out of the cutting a good view opens up of Carraghyn (a craggy place), Beinny Phott (or more correctly Beinn yn Oid meaning "turf peak", pronounced "penny pot") and Mullagh Ouyr. We head for the hut we could see earlier to cross the main road at Windy Corner. The hut is a marshal's shelter used in June and September when the road is closed to traffic and used for motorcycle racing. An emergency phone is located here and, indeed, at all of the shelters, and in winter many motorists have been thankful for their presence. The mountain road in winter is exposed to gales and snow and can be a very inhospitable place.

After crossing the road we walk over the cattle grid and head off down the Noble's Park Road, which was built in 1860 under the terms of the Disafforesting Act, following the sale of the island by the Duke of Athol to the Crown. Enjoy the views of the Laxey Valley and the range of hills to the north from Clagh Ouyr to Slieau Lhean, on the descent towards Glen Roy.

On joining the surfaced road, we continue down into the valley. Stop and look over the hedge to the right and you should see some stone piers on the opposite side of the Glen Roy valley, together with some ruined buildings. These are the surface remains of the Glen Roy Mine which was started in 1864 and was worked for about 25 years. The shaft reached a depth of 122 fathoms (732ft) and although some good lead and zinc blende was mined, it was not successful. The stone columns supported a timber aqueduct which provided water for the larger of two wheels used for pumping and crushing.

Passing Riverside in the bottom of the valley we have a steep climb up to the junction at Chibbyr Pheric (St Patrick's Well). Turning left, we aim for the hill ahead, keeping Axnfell Plantation on our left. Soon the road starts to descend towards Laxey and, as we leave the plantation, we are careful to take the footpath to the left, dropping steeply down into Laxey. Pause at the top to look up the Laxey Valley and at the Laxey Wheel sitting at the head of the Glen Mooar valley where all the mining activity took place. If time permits while in Laxey, visit the Mines Trail, but, if not, there will be other opportunities with other walks centred on Laxey.

On the way down into the village, be careful to follow the path so as to emerge in the centre of Laxey opposite the Commissioners' Offices. It is then a short walk to catch the tram to Douglas. Alternatively, take the No.15 bus at times when the railway is not running. Crossing the viaduct which spans the bottom end of the Glen Roy valley, stop and look at the Laxey Flour Mills and, on the opposite side of the road, the other gracefully curved viaduct which carries the tramway over the valley.

Douglas to the Strang

Those choosing to walk from Douglas to the start of *Stage 1* should leave the railway station by the clock tower and head off down Lord Street past the bus station, on past the Sea Terminal and onto the Loch Promenade. Walk on the seaward side from where you can see the full sweep of Douglas Bay. The boarding houses and hotels on this part of the promenade were all built on reclaimed land between 1876 and 1890 in response to the demands of tourism. The sunken gardens and elegant walkway were added much later in the 1930s.

Leaving Loch Promenade we come to the end of the gardens and the war memorial. This is a convenient place to cross the promenade onto the Harris Promenade and, ahead of us, is the façade of the Sefton Hotel and the Gaiety Theatre which was built in its present form around the turn of the century. The theatre is now the only survivor of many similar establishments which were built at the same period to provide both summer and year-round entertainment. Even if you are not a regular theatregoer, it is worth making a special effort to see one of the productions.

We walk under the colonnade to the Villa Marina, another

remnant from the past. This was the last of the major dance halls, but was used for many different functions and still plays host now and again to the big band revival of the present day.

We leave the promenade and walk up Broadway along the route of the Upper Douglas Cable Tramway *(described in the Douglas Town Trail)*, but carry straight on up Ballaquale Road, whereas the tramway veered to the left up York Road.

We pass St Ninian's Church and the secondary school, which is part of the Douglas High School in its expanded form, then go straight over the crossroads and along Ballanard Road to the next set of crossroads. Until very recently this was the point where Douglas stopped and country began, but recent development has encroached into the countryside.

We turn down Johnny Watterson's Lane to the village of Tromode or, as it is more correctly known, Cronkbourne

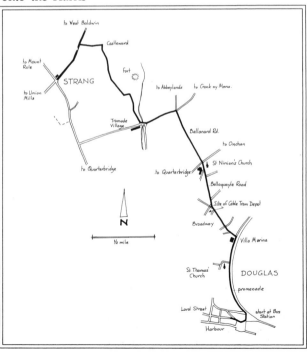

All change at Laxey for the Snaefell Mountain Railway

Village. You can see ahead a chimney just above the trees which marks the site of what is now a laundry. When the factory was first built it produced sail cloth and canvas. It was unusual in so far as it was the only large industry on the island to provide tied cottages and, as we enter the village, these can be seen on the left. They were also some of the earliest houses to be lit by electricity when the canvas company introduced and generated its own electricity in 1882.

Crossing over the bridge we must be careful not to miss the public footpath sign that takes us off to the right through what initially appears to be an industrial estate. However, it soon enters farmland and we make off towards Castleward Farm. As we head off up the hillside we can look down on the site of a fortified Iron Age homestead, *referred to in the historical section,* which is terraced and stands in a commanding position above the River Glass. Passing through

the farm we continue a short distance up the farm road to join the East Baldwin Road leading from the Strang. ❑

83

Laxey to Ramsey

*A 12-mile (19km) walk. You should allow
seven hours and it is advisable to take
refreshments. The walk takes in a number
of sites of industrial and archaeological
interest*

THE start point for the walk, which follows on from the previous route, is Laxey tram station. We leave the station, walking north, past the Mines Tavern and taking care to look out for the trams.

This pub was once the mine captain's house, built to overlook the washing floors of the Great Laxey Mines. We head off along the main road for a short distance before crossing it to walk along Mines Road.

To our left we can see the track of the Snaefell Mountain Railway starting its climb to the top of the island's highest peak. Ahead we can see the Great Laxey Wheel as we walk along "Ham and Egg Terrace". This row of mine workers' cottages earned its name from the reputation it had for providing visitors with good meals as they passed this way to see the Lady Isabella at the height of the pre-war tourist boom.

Passing the fire station, look across to the opposite bank of the river where you will see the entrance to the Cross Cut Adit (drift mine passage) which was dug in 1868 to connect the Main Adit to the Mines Yard and the changing rooms which were adjacent to the tunnel entrance. As we walk up the road to Agneash we pass the entrance to the Laxey Mines Trail. A short distance further up the hill is the lower end of the Browside Tramway, of which very little remains to indicate where it ran to the café which used to stand alongside the wheel.

This café was a wooden structure dating from about 1900, which was burnt down in 1985. The fire was extremely fierce and flames fanned by a strong wind at one time threatened the wheel itself. Firemen had to play water on the timber structure of the wheel to save it from damage.

Rounding the corner, we see the wheel at the top of the hill straight ahead of us. I always feel that this view shows the true scale of this magnificent structure as it towers above the houses either side of the road. We turn left before reaching the wheel and continue uphill to Agneash. As we approach the village we have a good view to our right of the area of the main mine working.

The building on the opposite side of the valley is the Engine House which housed a beam engine which was used for winding the "kibble", or bucket, carrying the ore out of the Engine and Welch shafts. It is generally thought that the engine was also used for pumping.

There is evidence, too, that a water wheel was built on the same site and the engine house was built around it, but industrial archaeologists were, at the time of writing, excavating the site to determine more about the precise function of this building which was central to the heart of the mine.

As we come into Agneash village, the hill ahead of us is Slieau Lhean (Broad mountain), while, to the right, is Slieau Ouyr (Brown mountain). Below us, the galleries of the Great Laxey Mine stretch beneath the village. To our right on the opposite hillside, north-east of the village, are the remains of some stone buildings which were the head works of

Dumbells shaft which, as described earlier, was the deepest shaft in the mine reaching a depth below the adit of 299 fathoms (552 metres). Slieau Lhean is 1,598 ft (461 metres) above sea level and the adit is about 325ft (100 metres) below us at Agneash.

With these facts in mind, we take a left fork by the village green and walk up the north side of the Laxey Valley, past Ballayolgane farm, heading for the Great Snaefell Mine which is located at the head of the valley. This is a classic glaciated valley, with its broad base, steep sides and steep head. On the left, across the valley, the line of the Snaefell Mountain Railway can be seen clinging to the side of Mullagh Ouyr (dun or brown summit) as it climbs to the top of Snaefell (snow mountain).

The road we are walking gradually deteriorates into a stony track and ends at the head of the valley at the site of the mines. Some surface remains exist, including the mine captain's house and a chimney from the original workings (*see*

Laxey mines washing floors around 1920 — the mine tramway ran to the adit through the tunnel on the right

picture on page 21). Most of the present surface features are brick-built and date only from the early 1950s, when the spoil heaps were re-worked by a company which was successful in retrieving some valuable metals by modern techniques.

The mine commenced work in 1856 and photographs show a large wheel located across the neck of the glen ahead of us near the chimney. Was this the original wheel from Laxey which was subsequently replaced by the Lady Isabella? Every indication is that it was the right size — 51ft as opposed to the 72ft 6ins of the Great Laxey Wheel. The date, too, is about right but I don't think we shall ever know with any certainty.

The mine was driven in a northerly direction for little more than half a mile and a much shorter distance south. There was one shaft, the top of which is visible to our right and surrounded by a substantial wall. The mine was sunk to a depth of 171 fathoms.

In May 1897 there was a disaster at the mine, in which 20 men lost their lives because of a fire at the 130-fathom level which filled the underground workings with poisonous gases. The mine continued working until 1908 and was productive throughout with galena (lead) and zinc blende the principal minerals.

Leaving the mine, we follow the signpost beside the mine captain's house up the flank of Clagh Ouyr (brown stone). The path is obscure and it is advisable to take a compass bearing of 45°. If in doubt, just head upwards!

As the going levels out we should pick up the line of an old track which we join and follow to the right in an easterly direction. Before heading off in the new direction, just look back the way we have come and see the extensive system of water collection across the head of the valley to provide the power for the water wheel.

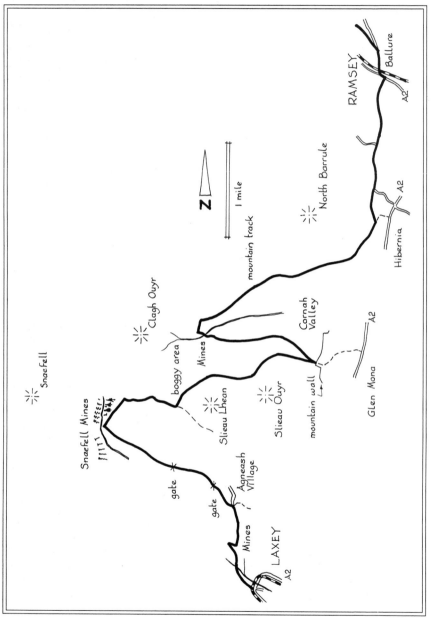

We shortly arrive at a boggy area in the saddle between Clagh Ouyr and Slieau Lhean through which we have to pick our way — this is all part of the fun of hill walking!

We have to take care here to make a left turn. There should be a signpost, but it is regularly blown down in winter. We skirt the north side of Slieau Lhean and Slieau Ouyr, following a clearly defined track, until we come to the mountain wall. All the time, the route commands a good view of the North Barrule ridge and North Barrule itself, while straight ahead we can see over Maughold with Maughold Head and the lighthouse in the distance.

At the mountain wall, we turn hard left and backtrack up the Cornah valley at a lower level. The track is not defined, but it is easy on a clear day to head up the valley using the clearly pointed outline of Clagh Ouyr as a guide. As the head of the valley comes into view, we can see the ruins of North Laxey Mines.

Above Snaefell Mines, overlooking the glaciated valley west of Laxey

Taking care crossing a deep gulley, we should now be able to see the line of the path as it follows an old mill race which fed water to a large wheel and the washing floors of the mine. The position of the wheel can be seen clearly as we approach the workings, where the water was carried across the valley in a timber aqueduct supported on three stone piers.

The remains of the washing floors are quite clearly seen as we drop down to the river which we have to cross — taking care not to get our feet wet… It is not a bad place to stop for a break as it is usually possible to find somewhere out of the wind.

The mine was started in the middle of last century. Two shafts were sunk — the north one eventually reached a depth of 174 fathoms and the south, 110 fathoms. By 1897, the mine had ceased working, and, although it had produced 1,763 tons of lead ore, it never recovered its cost.

Suitably refreshed, we strike up the other side of the valley by way of a sheepfold to pick up a clearly-defined track which takes us back down the valley below North Barrule, heading for a ruined house in the distance. The ruin is Park Llewellyn House and as we pass it we continue through a gate onto a more defined road between two stone hedges. All the time we skirt Barrule under the stone crags of the east face which are frequented by a pair of ravens. The name Barrule is of Norse derivation and is connected with the ancient duty of watch and ward which discontinued in 1815.

We join a surfaced roadway at Hibernia which we follow for almost half a mile, then going straight on where the road veers left. The view over the northern plain shows the fertile land of the northern parishes and the Bridge Hills in the distance, with just a glimpse of the Point of Ayre lighthouse at the northernmost tip of the island.

Ramsey, our destination, is just below us and we quickly descend the old Ramsey-Douglas road, which is steep and quite difficult to walk down.

We finally join the main road to Ramsey at Ballure and follow it over the tram crossing into the town. If we follow Waterloo Road for about a quarter of a mile, we shall be at the tram station for our return to Douglas. ❏

Ramsey to Sulby

A seven-mile (11kms) route along the northern fringe of the Manx uplands, offering commanding views across the northern plain and passing the Iron Age fort at Cronk Sumark. This stage can be combined with the following one for those not wishing to break the journey at Sulby

FROM Ramsey station, walk along Queens Pier Road, past the bus station into Parliament Square. Continuing through the Square, cross the Sulby River on the Bowring Road bridge. You can look across to the right and appreciate a good view of Ramsey harbour, with the shipyard and the swing bridge in the distance. Looking to the left, across the river, you can see Sky Hill, up which you will soon be climbing.

Continue up Bowring Road to its junction with Jurby Road opposite St Olave's Church. A short distance further up the road is the Grove Museum, *described in the Ramsey Town Trail*. However, you should turn left along Jurby Road for a little way before turning left again down Gardeners Lane to the Sulby River.

Crossing the river by the White bridge, pause and consider this part of the river which is still tidal here, and sheltered from the open sea. There is no doubt why this area was a favoured landing place for the Vikings in their longboats. Carry on along the road until you join the main road from Ramsey to Peel, and turn right.

You must walk along the road for about quarter of a mile under the foot of Sky Hill. Look for the Millennium Way signs at the foot of Sky Hill (map reference MR432944), turn left and follow the signs up the hill.

Sky Hill — originally called Scacafell, from the Scandinavian Skogarfjall, meaning wooded hill — was the site of

a battle in 1079 when Godred Crovan overcame the Manx after two earlier unsuccessful attempts. He became the first King of Mann and his descendants continued to rule the island until 1266 when the island kingship transferred to the Scottish kingdom.

The Vikings are generally recognised as having occupied the island from a period one hundred years earlier than the date of the battle of Sky Hill and so, in 1979, the Isle of Man Government celebrated its Millennium. As part of those celebrations, the Government created a long distance footpath over the route of the ridgeway from the ancient landing place at Ramsey to Castletown and the fertile southern farmland. The long distance footpath was appropriately named *The Millennium Way* and is described in more detail later.

On the way up Sky Hill, stop after leaving the plantation to look over the northern plain from the bold white shape of Jurby Church to your left, round to the Point of Ayre lighthouse, which is at the northernmost part of the island and can be just seen above the Bride Hills. The large building which can also be seen near to Jurby Church is a hanger in which an exciting airship project is being undertaken.

Carry on over Park ny Earkan until you reach the top mountain gate. Turn right and follow the defined track on the mountain side of the road which leads into an unsurfaced road between two hedges. This is the Rhullick Road —

meaning cemetery, or churchyard, road relating to a keeill (early chapel) at the Nappin — and it is followed to join the main road near the Ginger Hall.

Turn left on reaching the road and follow the Claddagh Road to Old Sulby Village. A short distance along the road, as we pass beneath Cronk Sumark, look for the cream coloured fingerpost giving access to the top of the hill and its Iron Age fortification, remains of which can still be seen. The climb to the top is steep but worth the effort, not only for the archaeological interest but also the surprising view which makes it clear why it was chosen as a fort site.

Returning to the road, continue through the Claddagh alongside the Sulby River to Old Sulby Village. To return to Douglas, walk the short distance to Sulby Glen and catch the No.5 or 6 bus. ❏

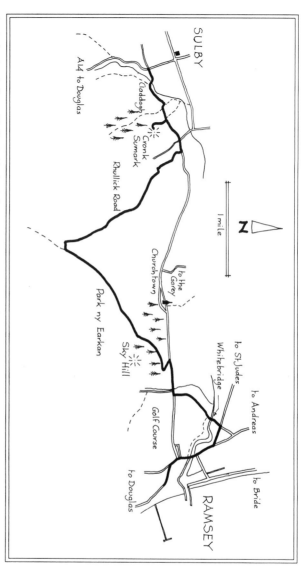

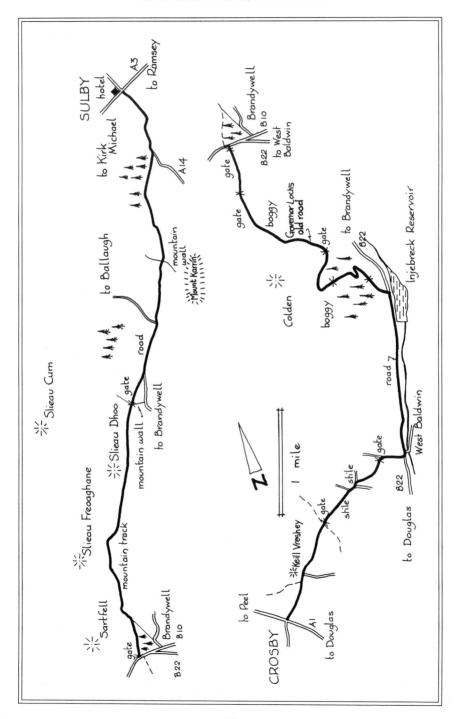

Sulby to Crosby

A 13-mile (21kms) walk through the Michael Hills and West Baldwin. Allow seven hours. It is advisable to take refreshments. The route affords good views of the island with some archaeological interest

THIS is another walk in the northern half of the island embracing the hills overlooking the west coast. From Douglas, take the No. 5 or 6 bus to Sulby Glen crossroads.

Cross the road, passing the village shop and head up Glen Road. Those who have stayed overnight in Sulby join the route at the village green. After passing a series of bends, we arrive at a small collection of houses and find our track leading off to the right between them. This heads off through Ballacuberagh Plantation, quickly gaining height and gradually emerging on the western slopes of Mount Karrin and the back of Ballaugh Mountain. As we join the open moorland, we are still on an easily followed track and soon join a surfaced road which we follow for about a quarter of a mile. Here we start to lose our view over the north, seeing instead the very obvious landmark of Jurby Church on the coast to our right.

We must be careful not to miss our way here as we leave the surfaced road at a shallow angle to the right (map reference 363904) on a white coloured stony, unsurfaced road which quickly degenerates into a rutted track as it joins and follows the mountain boundary wall. We pass Slieau Dhoo (Black Mountain) on our right and can make a detour to the top to picnic. There is a stony depression which provides shelter, as well as an interesting pond, and there is a good view ahead of Slieau Freoghane (generally accepted as meaning Bilberry Mountain) and Sartfell.

Making our way back to the track, we continue south west with views opening to our left of the Sulby Reservoir, which was only completed in 1983. Beyond it is Snaefell, while the pointed peak of North Barrule can be seen to the far left. The valley immediately below is Druidale. We continue along the mountain wall until it turns left and we follow it as the track becomes quite difficult to walk along. The view ahead now changes and we see Slieau Maggle and Colden (from the Scandinavian Kollrinn, meaning the top summit) ahead.

We join the surfaced road at a gate and take a left turn for a short distance before turning right on the track which passes the sheep pens on the side of Slieau Maggle (this means literally the "mountain of the testicles", so named because, traditionally, lambs were brought here to be castrated and sheep pens are still used in the same location). The way is known as Governor Loch's road and, although metalled and stonepitched, it was never completed. This is a pity, because, as we shall see, it commands views of some magnificent scenery. It remains a public road but, because it is now unsuitable for traffic, we find some unusual road signs apparently in the middle of nowhere.

We follow the road to a mountain wall and gate. Passing through the gate, we must strike off left along the wide road with its hedges on either side. It is usually very wet in the middle where it is impossible to walk, except in winter when it is frozen. We must pick our way along the bank on the right for about half a mile after which the road becomes more obvious and firmer under foot, being cut on a ledge in the hillside.

Skirting the shoulder of Colden, we have a superb view of Injebreck Hill and valley. We can make much better time now, and the walking is easy as we swing round by the top of Colden Plantation and pass through some ornamental gate posts which are remnants of the enclosures made by the Commissioners of Woods and Forest in 1860.

We now enter the natural amphitheatre of the cirque on the east side of Colden, formed when the great ice sheet which covered the Irish Sea basin retreated to leave numerous lakes in locations such as this. The cirque is more noticeable from a distance, but it is always a sheltered spot which forms a sun-trap on a good summer's day and is normally occupied only by a few sheep.

We cross over a stone bridge — now, sadly, partly destroyed by floodwater — and head along the road for the plantation, which commands a superb view of Carraghyn (craggy place) ahead of us. The road is very boggy here again and we must watch our step as we enter the plantation, trying to avoid going in over the top of our boots! If it is very wet, try up to the right under the trees. Fortunately, after a short distance, we can again enjoy the walk, down through Colden Plantation into the West Baldwin Valley.

Eventually, we shall come out on the West Baldwin road opposite the Injebreck Reservoir, built by the Douglas Corporation and completed in 1905. The undertaking was designed to meet the demands of the future and was without doubt extremely far-sighted, only recently needing to be supplemented.

We turn right and walk alongside the reservoir to West Baldwin village. As we approach the bridge at West Baldwin, we can see to the left traces of the formation of the reservoir tramway and another of the quarries used in the building of the dam. Just after the bridge, we join the Millennium Way again and, following the waymarkers, walk through Ballagrawe and Ballalough, crossing a stone stile into a lane which we follow for a short while before crossing a ladder stile into fields on the eastern flank of Greeba.

Enjoying superb views to the left towards Douglas, we head for the saddle between Greeba on the right and the small hill on the left — Cronk ny Moghlane or Mucaillyn (hill of the sows). The Millennium Way crosses over a track and down towards Crosby which is the finish of this walk. From here a No. 5, 6 or 6A bus will take the walker back to Douglas.

At Ballaharry, where the track joins the surfaced road, we can make a detour into the adjoining field to view the remains of the Celtic Keeill Vreshey, one of the many examples of Celtic Christianity which abound in the island. The keeill was later known as the Chapel of St Bridget. The Norse were eventually converted to Christianity, and King Olaf II — great grandson of Godred Crovan, the first King of Mann — granted land in the vicinity of the keeill to the Priory of Whithorn, in Galloway.   ❑

Crosby to Peel

*An 11-mile (18km) mainly moorland walk
by way of Slieau Ruy and Rhenass. Allow
four and a half hours. Full facilities
available at Peel and plenty of time to
view the castle*

STARTING at Douglas, take a No. 5 or 6 bus to Crosby Church, getting off at the stop on the Glenvine side of the church. To reach this point from the end of the last stage you have to walk half a mile along the A1 towards Douglas, passing the parish church of Marown (the only parish in the island which does not touch the coast). Then turn left, uphill, opposite the Manx Motor Museum along the Glenvine Road. The museum houses a private collection of interesting vehicles, including many early American ones.

Follow the road past Ballawilleykilley (Killey's fold farm), crossing the Mount Rule road at Corvonagh, to continue to the top of Cronk ny Moghlane. The road takes a sharp turn to the right at the top of the hill and it is worth stopping to admire the view across the central valley. We can see the lesser known hills that form the south side of the valley. From Douglas on the left, the Carnane is prominent and easily distinguished by the TV transmitter on its peak; the Mount and Slieau Chiarn (Hill of the Lord) are almost ahead of us; and Creg y Whuallian and Slieau Whallian (Aleyn's mountain) lie to our right.

As we round the next corner, another panorama of island hills greets us and it is time to get the map out and identify them all and see where we travelled on the previous walk, with the East Baldwin valley below us. Carrying on uphill, the path gets steeper and rougher as we climb the bulk of Slieau Ruy. We come to the bottom mountain gate and, as we walk on easier ground, we have a good view of Colden and the Creg over Eairy Vane and Eairy ne Sooie, the place names showing that these farms developed

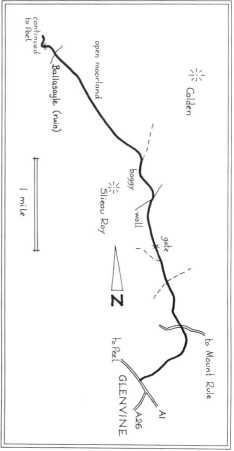

93

from earlier *shielings* (summer pastures).

After passing the top mountain gate, we find ourselves on the open mountain but still following a defined track. Half a mile from the gate we negotiate a boggy area, but shortly after this we have to take care not to miss the signpost which shows where we must go to get to Rhenass. A compass bearing of 310° should get us over the shoulder between Slieau Ruy and Lhargee Ruy, otherwise go off at right angles (left) to the path, but resist the temptation to follow the very old track heading off left.

There are markers which, if we are lucky, we should pick up. Once over the top we should see the shape of a large stone sheep pen characteristic of the old crown and common lands, and that is where we are heading. The pen is in the shape of a letter "D" and we want to walk along the straight wall of it to pick up the line of an old track which will lead us over the open moorland to Rhenass. There are concrete markers on the line of the path, but again, if there is any doubt, head for the dip in the line of the hills ahead and eventually a white house will come into view — the perfect landmark.

As we walk across this area, which is on the western flank of Lhargee Ruy (the red slope), we can see to the left the prominent shape of Corrin's Folly on Corrin's Hill above Peel and, closer to hand, the head of Glen Helen, one of the island's prettiest National Glens. Approaching the end of the moorland, cross to the right hand side of the track which quickly develops into a gully, and aim for the gate in the corner, which is really the line of the road, now more apparent between hedges. After a short distance we turn right through a gate past the ruins of Ballasayle (Sayle's farm) and can see, as we pass, one of the best surviving examples of a horse mill, in which the millstone was turned by a horse tethered to a pole. These mills, with their characteristic circular platfrom around which the horse would walk, were more common on hillsides where water was scarce in summer.

We follow the track down to the stream which we can cross on the step-

Journey's end — the harbour at Peel, with the castle in the background

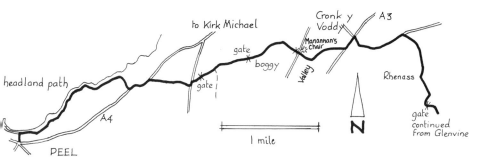

ping stones. We cross over the little stone bridge at Mullen Rhenass and follow the road to the junction with the Little London Road, and turn left to follow the surfaced road to Cronk y Voddy (hill of the dog) crossroads. We go left here on the main road — this is one of those areas which is a no-go zone on certain days in June and September, because of motorcycle racing.

After a short distance, we pick up the sign on the other side of the road and walk across an unusual and inconspicuous upland valley, as we head for the Staarvey Road (Staarvey meaning a rough, shallow ford), passing the mysterious early Iron Age feature known as Mannanan's Chair. We cross the road through the gate and follow this very wet muddy track past Lherghycholvine, passing the remains of a number of tholtans (abandoned farmsteads) giving silent homage to a past way of life. The view over Peel, our ultimate destination, is rewarding as we descend to the Knocksharry Road and cross it, taking the road through the farm at Lhergydhoo (the black slope). We pass over the old railway line that used to run to Ramsey before we meet the coast road.

Turning left, we walk a short distance along this road before going through a white stile on the right to take the headland path to Peel, arriving on the promenade having enjoyed views of the castle on St Patrick's Isle. Return to Douglas by the No.5 bus. ❑

95

Peel to Port Erin

A 13½-mile (23km) walk. Allow seven and a half hours. Advisable to take refreshments. Mostly a scenic route — some interesting geological formations and industrial archaeological remains

FROM Douglas, take the No. 5, 6 or 6A bus to Peel and make your way down to the bridge at the head of the harbour.

We set off along the West Quay towards the castle, but after a short distance walk up the concrete ramp on the left and head off up Peel Hill. The track turns above Fenella Beach, but we leave it and walk up the ridge of Peel Hill, pausing at the first rocky outcrop to look back over the castle. When we reach the top of Peel Hill we can see a saddle and ridge continuing to the top of Corrin's Hill, with its 50ft folly, built in 1806 by one Thomas Corrin as a memorial to his family. He, his wife and child are buried nearby.

We have a choice to go that way or follow a track leading off to the right, on the seaward side of Corrin's Hill. I'm going that way because I think it is more interesting.

Shortly after making off along this path, pass through a stile in the wall. The path is on a ledge in the hillside and as we pass the rock on our left, note the drill holes where the ledge has been cut by man. We are following the oldest recorded tramroad in the island which was almost certainly a horse tramway with wooden rails. Information is scarce, but it was used for hauling slate from an incline at the quarry on Contrary Head, clearly seen in the distance, to a similar incline on the other side of the hill which lowered the stone to harbour level. The views from this path are quite stunning and as we walk south we may hear the guillemots in their colony on Cashtal Mooar (the big castle), a large rock just below us.

As we pass Contrary Head the alternative route over the top of the hill joins our path and we make our way through the stile to follow the coastal path to Glen Maye, with views to the south, of Cronk ny Irree Laa in the distance, and in the foreground, Niarbyl (in Manx, *Yn Arbyl*, "the tail" — a perfect description of the rocks running out to sea at this point). See if you can see the Bonnet Rock as you pass down this section of coast. It is quite distinct and is in the middle of Traie Cabbag (the wild cabbage shore).

As we leave the coast and head inland we are walking on the lip of the gorge of Glen Maye (the yellow glen) and we gradually make our way down to the glen itself. Cross the road and into the glen path by the wheel case of the North Foxdale Mine which closed in 1870. A plaque on this structure describes a little of the history of the wheel which was named the Mona-Erin and was 34ft in diameter.

We can enjoy the walk up the glen — there are choices, but we shall take the lower path alongside the river, making a short detour to view the waterfall.

We climb up the path to leave the glen and join the main road, turning right down to the bottom of the hill, then taking the left fork along the Sound Road with the stream running parallel to it. We quickly start to climb up a very rough track between high hedges. In places, the going underfoot is very dif-

The site of the hermitage at Lag ny Killey

ficult across sloping slate slabs. The tricky bit is only short and we soon gain better ground, emerging almost on the top of Dalby Mountain. We follow the track on open moorland until we join a surfaced roadway. Ahead and behind us are good views of the west coast of the island.

We head off left on the road (the A27) for a short way until we arrive at a triangular parking area (map reference 232767) with a track leading to Eary Cushlin. We have to be careful to take to the moorland. It is signposted and a track has been cut through the heather. We head for the corner of Slieau Mooar Plantation and continue more or less in a straight line on a heading of 195° until we reach a wooden stile over the mountain wall to join an unsurfaced road. From the point at which we left the Eary Cushlin track, it is possible to make a two-mile detour to visit the Keeill Lag ny Killey, a tiny Christian hermitage perched on a slight platform on the plunging coastline. To make this detour, carry straight on to the Eary Cushlin

hostel, and continue along the track until it diminishes to a path which descends 500ft until you come upon the remains of the chapel in a small natural bowl. Whatever your religious convictions, it is hard not to admire the resilience of the hermit priest, cultivating his tiny field. The little chapel was built some time in the fifth or sixth century and enjoyed a stunning outlook across the sea to Ireland. It was last used for a funeral 100 years ago, when the corpse was carried down the steep hill strapped to the back of a pony. To rejoin the main route, retrace your steps towards Eary Cushlin, but strike off right before there at the point where the Manx Coastal Path crosses at right angles and heads for the summit of Cronk ny Irrey Laa.

If you don't want to lose all that height, turn left after the stile and climb to the top of the hill where the track rejoins the road (now the A36). All the time, we enjoy a good view to the left of South Barrule (hill of watch and ward) and, nearer to us, the brown slope of Cronk Fedjag (hill of the plover). Going straight

97

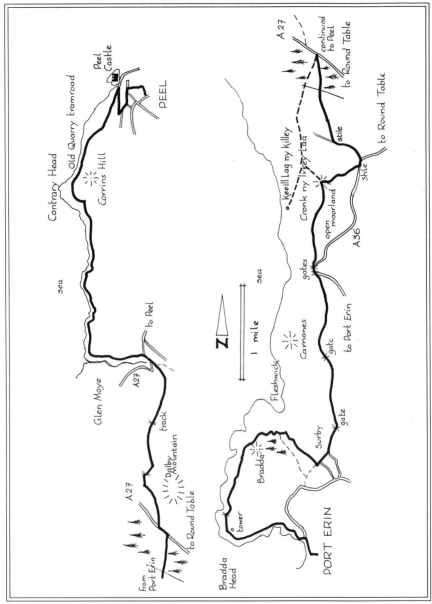

along the surfaced road again for a short distance, we go through the kissing gate on the right and head up the broad track to the top of Cronk ny Arrey Laa, or, more appropriately, Cronk ny Irree Laa. Unfortunately, both spellings have dif-

ferent meanings — the first means "the hill of the day watch", a remnant from the times when it was the duty of the Captain of the Parish to ensure that a day watch and a night watch were kept, a practice which persisted until 1815.

The coastline plunges from the spectacular summit of Cronk ny Irree Laa

wick, Bradda, and the Calf of Man beyond. We follow the path in the heather down to the Sloc (pit or hollow) from where there is a fine view over the south east of the island, with Castletown and Langness peninsula in the far distance.

We skirt under Burroo Mooar (big rocky hillock) along the edge of a gully joining the Sloc road beside the sheep pens. We don't stay on the road at all, simply going out of one gate and in the next. The picnic tables provide a convenient spot for a rest and refreshment. Following the wide track, we start to descend towards Surby. Superb views of the south of the island unfold as we go, with the Calf of Man in the far distance. We come off the mountain through a gate and join the Surby road and come back to

The latter spelling is more acceptable and perpetuated in folklore as "the hill of the dawn", when fishermen used the hill as a fishing mark and the sun as a signal to shoot their nets.

The huge summit cairn is a prehistoric burial mound, probably dating from the early Bronze Age, around 1500BC.

The summit of Cronk ny Irree Laa commands even better views of the coast and, in particular, to the south, overlooking the Sloc and the very distinctive shape of Lhiattee ny Beinee, with Flesh-

civilisation. At the bottom of the hill at Surby, we turn right, taking the road to Fleshwick (green creek) and again we are treated to some beautiful views of the island, particularly as we approach the beach with the high cliffs on the right under the Carnanes. I think this spot is at its best in winter with a full westerly gale churning the sea into a seething frenzy.

We don't quite get to the beach, however, because we rejoin the coastal footpath and follow the waymarkers up the back of Bradda (broad headland).

Milner's Tower on Bradda Head, seen from Port Erin harbour, with the old breakwater in the foreground

The views from the top are worth all the effort, particularly the one back over the big bay, with Cronk ny Irree Laa sweeping down to the sea and the tail of rocks at Niarbyl, and, in the distance, Corrin's Hill, where we started this walk.

The coastal path from here to Port Erin is mostly downhill and we head for Milner's Tower in the distance. The tower was built by public subscription in 1871 to the memory of William Milner, the Liverpool safe-maker who lived in Port Erin and was a benefactor of the village, helping build a breakwater in the middle of last century to shelter the harbour from westerly gales. If you look carefully at the tower, you will see it is built in the shape of a key.

Before we reach the tower, stop at the fence leading onto Bradda Head and look over the cliff to see the surface remains of the North Bradda Mines at the foot of the cliff, opposite the rock jutting out in the sea. With the aid of binoculars, you may be able to make out some green copper staining on the cliff.

We have a choice of paths through Bradda to Port Erin but we will follow the one closest to the sea and may, if we are careful, see the surface remains of the South Bradda Mine. On the way into Port Erin, we pass the bay and stony beach at Spaldrick. Another Scandinavian word, Spjaldirk, gives the origin of the name and means square beach. All of the beach or inlet names ending with "ick" are of Norse origin and were originally landing places.

Making our way along the top promenade to the railway station, we should be in time for the last train back to Douglas, after paying a visit to the Railway Museum.

The museum has among its exhibits the Manx Northern Railway locomotive, *Caledonia*, and one of the six-wheeled coaches favoured by that company. The largest loco owned by the Isle of Man Railway Company, *Mannin*, is also on display with the Royal saloon. Other exhibits are varied from time to time and there are many photographs on display.

The steam trains only run in the summer season and, regrettably, the museum is only open during the same period. So, for the rest of the year, it is back to Douglas on a No.1 or 1A bus from the bus station which is next to the railway station. ❏

Port Erin to Castletown

The first part of the walk, via Bay Fine, Calf Sound and the Chasms to Port St Mary, is 7¹/₂ miles (12kms). Allow four hours. Refreshment available in summer at the Sound and at weekends in winter. Scenic route with geological and archaeological interest. The extension to Castletown adds six miles (9.5km), or two to three hours

IF YOU have never been to the Isle of Man before, this walk should be a good introduction for you. In summer, this route can be idyllic, and for the novice walker there is a choice that allows you to break the walk into two sections, returning to your start by bus.

From Douglas, take the steam train from the station at the head of the harbour all the way to Port Erin, which is the terminus of the line. It is worth taking some time out, if we take the first train of the day, to look around the Railway Museum. Out of season we shall have to travel south on a No.1 bus.

We leave the station and walk down Strand Road to the Lower Promenade, and head off towards the pier and lifeboat station. We can cross the road here and take the coastal path up behind the Liverpool University Marine Biological Station (open to the public). In early summer, we can easily look over the wall above the buildings and if we are lucky we should see some young herring gulls on the nest.

On the elevated area behind the lifeboat house, can be seen the workshops and engine shed of the railway that was built to serve the construction of the Port Erin breakwater. This was the site of the block-making yard. The wide arched doorway is indicative of the gauge of the line.

The breakwater was completed in 1876 but this giant structure was severely damaged during a gale in 1881 and was finally demolished by the sea in 1884.

Through the stile at the end of the wall, we can look across the bay towards Bradda Head and see the remains of the South Bradda mines which produced lead and copper but were last worked in the 1880s. Looking south, we can see Bay Fine and the Calf of Man in the distance. As we climb the path, we pass close to a fulmar colony. The climb is quite steep but the view from the top both ahead of us, and behind over Port Erin and Bradda, is worth a pause for a breather.

The path follows the top of the cliff along Jirra Point before dropping to skirt the hollow above Bay Fine. We shall keep to the slightly higher path which follows the top of an old sod hedge, curving above the bay. The view back towards Port Erin is quite beautiful but, to my mind, even better in winter in the teeth of a westerly gale.

Over the top we must be careful not to miss the path, which is not well marked. We walk diagonally across the open top of the headland, with a striking view of the Calf Island as we cross a boundary wall by a stile before descending the now clearly defined path above Aldrick (meaning the Old People's Creek). Note particularly the fissured rocks, more of which later.

Ahead of us is an unusual feature known locally as Jacob's Rock, which forms the foreground to our view of Calf Island. We can look down to the stony beach at Aldrick at this point before we climb up a steep section of the path between rocks and then down along the grassy edge of the cliff to the Calf Sound and a welcome break at the Sound Café for delicious home-made quiche and Manx *bonnag* — a fruit scone made with buttermilk. The café overlooks the Sound itself, with Kitterland and Calf Island, which is now uninhabited and is a bird sanctuary under the care of the Manx National Trust. If we are lucky, we may hear seals calling from the Cletts, a series of rocks to the left of the Calf.

In the summer you can get a 1A bus back from here, but take care as they only run every hour during the afternoon.

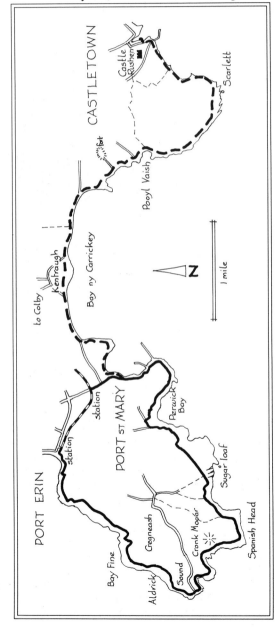

For the rest of us, it is time to press on, suitably refreshed. We follow the path along the parade, which is the open grass area, and make our way around Burroo Ned, overlooking Baie ny Breechyn (The Bay of the Breeches) so named because of the rock which splits the bay into two legs. We cross the stream, now made easy by a small bridge, to climb in earnest to the top of Cronk Mooar (which just means big hill, although it has another name, Cronk y Feeagh, which means hill of the ravens. I prefer the latter, as a pair of ravens range between here and Black Head). The view south from the top is magnificent, with the Sound separating the Calf of Man from the Isle of Man and the small islet of Kitterland between the two.

The Calf of Man from Aldrick, with Jacob's Rock ahead, over the stile

We continue our walk past Spanish Head and Black Head. The path is close to the cliff edge at this point, and although quite safe, children should be closely supervised, particularly in poor visibility. Looking south, we can see the forbidding back face of Spanish Head with the tail of the Calf of Man behind it terminating in the Burroo, a quite distinctive rock which has a hole through it. We should also be able to see the Chicken Rock lighthouse which is no longer used, following a fire in 1960.

The lighthouse was built in 1875 to replace two earlier lights built in 1818 to a design of Robert Stevenson's (grandfather of Robert Louis Stevenson). Now it has been replaced by a modern lighthouse built on the Calf in 1968. All the lighthouses are still there and a day trip to the Calf from Port Erin or Port St Mary should not be missed.

Looking north, ahead of us, we overlook Baie ny Stackey, taking its name from the Stack, or Sugar Loaf Rock, which we shall see shortly. The path is easily followed and, as we close up on the cliffs ahead, we see that they are

fissured, but more so than at Aldrick. Here, they are more appropriately called the Chasms, and were created by severe earth movements. We head for the disused building (now a shelter) and cross the boundary wall by a stile and, opposite the shelter, go through a small gate which gives access to the Chasms, and also to a small hill fort on the southern edge of the cliff. Take great care when viewing the cracks in the rock which range from a few inches to several feet in width and extend almost to sea level.

We take the path along the wall to the left as we look to sea, and following it to a kissing gate. As we pass through, we overlook the Sugar Loaf Rock and again the path is very close to the cliff edge. From here we strike off diagonally to the left to join a defined track which we can see clearly ahead of us. After a short distance crossing fields we join a surfaced roadway which takes us towards Port St Mary, which we can now see ahead of us.

As we come into civilisation at Glen Chass, we take a right fork in the road, passing the dip at the Glen to take a

The Chasms

footpath, clearly marked, through another kissing gate, crossing the grounds of the former Perwick Bay Hotel, now replaced by two apartment blocks. Follow the signs through yet another kissing gate to follow the coast around Perwick Bay and Kallow Point.

Arriving at the harbour, you can, if you wish, get the No.1 bus back to Douglas — it stops next to the Albert Hotel. Alternatively, you can walk another mile up Port St Mary High Street, past Chapel Bay, which I think is the nicest beach in the island, to catch the train back from the station, waiting in the Station Hotel next door until it comes.

Walkers on our round-island walk should make the following diversion from Port St Mary to stay overnight at Castletown before starting *Stage 8*, although, if the pleasures of the Albert Hotel have been too great, you might have to get the bus anyway!

Opposite the Albert, take the immediate left below the High Street and walk the landward side of the harbour, beside the converted warehouses and chandleries which give a hint of the past

importance of Port St Mary as a fishing and boat-building port. The road soon finishes and you will find yourself on an elevated walkway. The Cain-Karran footpath gives the best entry to Chapel Beach. You must continue along the Lower Promenade and round Gansey Point to join the promenade at Baie ny Carrickey (the bay of the rock). The walk along the wide sweep of Bay ny Carrickey is perhaps a little monotonous so you can take to the shore here, but it is stony at Kentraugh and heavy going.

However, it is worth persisting because you soon get to the interesting bit where the path travels around the promontory. Follow the coastal path signs and you will be rewarded with much bird life — plovers, gulls, curlews, choughs (I have seen as many as 30 in a flock here), oystercatchers, sanderlings, herons — the list is endless. A short distance inland stand the remains of one of two Iron Age forts, as the path continues through Poyll Vaaish farm and on towards Scarlett.

The quarry at Poyll Vaaish provided marble which was used to make steps at St Paul's Cathedral, London. There are some superb rock formations at Scarlett (from the Scandinavian Skarfakluft, meaning cormorant's cleft), including the volcanic plug which forms Scarlett Rock and is accessible at low water. Its basalt formation is quite distinct.

As you round the point, you pass the remains of lime kilns, a quarry and a small jetty near a ruined weighbridge from where lime was exported. Ahead of you is Castletown, dominated by the castle, which was built in its present form during the 14th century, although it is clear that some form of defensive works existed in Norse times. ❏

Castletown to Douglas

A ten-mile (15km) walk via Santon and Kewaigue. Allow four and a half hours. Refreshments advised. A mostly coastal walk, with much historical interest

TAKE the train to Castletown, or catch the No.1 or 1A bus and get off in the square right opposite the castle. Castletown was the ancient capital of the island and it shows in the architecture of the buildings which remain in the immediate vicinity of the castle. Note particularly the one-fingered clock on the keep which is guaranteed to confuse.

We go off to the right, past the police station and cross the harbour by the swing bridge to turn right into Douglas Street. We pass the Nautical Museum which is worth a visit *(see Castletown Town Trail)*. Those catching the steam train from Douglas will join the walk here, having turned left out of the station road and followed the road straight on past the roundabout and bearing right on to the promenade.

We continue on the coastline, taking the right fork to join Castletown Promenade and pause at Hango Hill, opposite King William's College, a public school founded in 1830. It was designed by the architect John Welch and largely funded out of the Bishop Barrow Trust.

The history attached to the fate of William Christian who was shot at Hango Hill in 1663 is long and involved. Christian owned Ronaldsway farm, now the site of the airport, and was appointed Receiver General to the Lord of Mann, James VII, Earl of Derby, also known as "the Great Stanley". He fought for the Royalists against Cromwell, but was captured and executed at Bolton. In an effort to save her husband's life, the Countess, who had been left in residence at Castle Rushen, offered to surrender the island to the Roundheads. This so incensed Christian, who was known as Illiam Dhone (swarthy William) that he led a force in opposition to the Countess who then surrendered to Christian. He then agreed in his turn to surrender the island to Parliament, provided it could retain its ancient laws and liberties.

The Sugar Loaf Rock, left, and Scarlett Rock

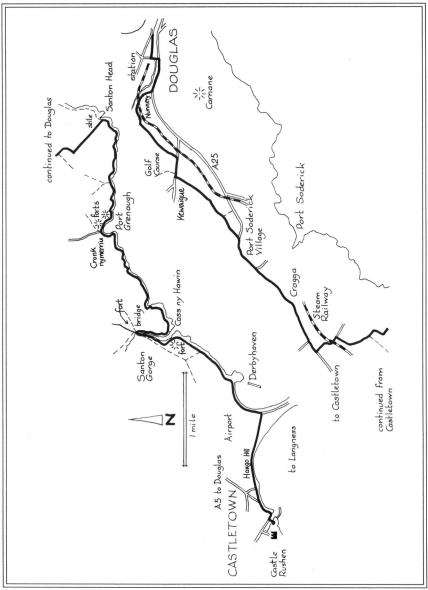

He eventually became Governor of the island under the Commonwealth, but was arrested two years later for misappropriating public funds. His undoing came after the Restoration when, believing it safe to return to the island, he was arrested, tried under the direction of the eighth Earl, Charles, son of the Great Earl, and executed on this spot.

Continue past the airport to Derbyhaven. This ancient landing place, a naturally sheltered harbour, took its name from the second Earl of Derby who landed here in 1507. We soon reach the headland at Cass ny Hawin (foot of the river) and from the site of an iron age promontory fort which has also revealed traces of habitation from Norse times, we can enjoy a superb view up the east coast to Santon Head. The archaeological site is on a raised beach of great geological interest, indicating the higher sea level which once prevailed.

We have to follow the coastal path to negotiate the crossing of the Santon Gorge by a footbridge, and, turning sharp right to follow the river bank, we climb through an avenue of trees to the path on the cliff top. The view ahead, to the north, extends to Santon Head, and, as we round the first headland into Port Soldrick, or Jackdaw, Bay, there is a large cave on the opposite headland. The path runs above this on the way to Port Grenagh. Here we cross the head of the beach and continue up the opposite headland on the coastal path, stopping at Cronk ny Merriu, where the remains of yet another promontory fort also exhibit signs of later Norse occupation.

We continue in a northerly direction, crossing the inlet near the Baltic Rock to emerge on the broad back of Santon Head. We must watch out for a public right of way sign and gate (map reference 336705) which takes us over fields inland to join a farm road through Meary Veg (Meary being derived from a Scandinavian word meaning border land) to join a surfaced road leading to Balnahowe, near the steam railway line. The view south clearly shows the peninsula of Langness and St Michael's Isle, with the chapel of St Michael dating from the early 12th century and the Derby Fort built to protect the harbour of Derbyhaven and to defend it against the forces of Cromwell during the English Civil War.

Turning left at the road we cross the railway and walk to the Old Castletown Road, turning right towards Douglas.

We shall stay on the road for about a mile. As we descend the hill, we pass Crogga House, which takes its name from the winding river which feeds the lake at the bottom of the hill. As we arrive at Port Soderick village we must look for the right of way sign to direct us along the ancient highway to Kewaigue. Its entrance is obscured by new building but it leads off to the left (map reference 347737) and we follow it through Middle Farm to join the main road opposite Kewaigue school.

We turn right and walk down the hill alongside Douglas golf course, turning left at the bottom of the hill before reaching the railway bridge to follow the Middle River towards Douglas and the Pulrose Power Station which can be seen ahead. The power station was built in 1929 to supplement an earlier one on the quayside in Douglas. It has been extended and modernised several times. The original station used steam-driven turbine generator sets and the latest extension to the station was opened in 1989 by HRH the Duke of Edinburgh. It uses the very latest type of diesel generating sets and is the principal generating station for the island.

Near to the station we come to a small bridge crossing the stream which we must cross to the right. The track we are now following is an old funeral road leading from Douglas to Old Kirk Braddan church. It passes through the Nunnery Estate, an area which is full of history. It takes its name from the Nunnery of St Bridget, the origins of which are uncertain. Only the chapel of the old nunnery remains.

The present house at the Nunnery was built in 1830 and occupied by the Taubman family and, prior to that, by Deemster Heywood. A Deemster is the equivalent in the Manx Judiciary system to an English High Court Judge.

The Deemster's son, Peter, was born at the Nunnery in 1773 and was a mid-

The rewarding view on completing the Manxman's Meander — Steam Packet ferries mv Peveril and mv Channel Entente (now King Orry) at Douglas Sea Terminal

shipman to Captain Bligh of the Bounty. Heywood was only 14 at the time of the famous mutiny but, although condemned to death as a mutineer, he was subsequently pardoned as a result of his sister's intervention through Queen Charlotte. He later rose to the rank of Captain.

As we walk along the old road, a gap in the wall enables us to view an obelisk commemorating the Crimean War. We emerge next to the ornate gatehouse adjacent to the Nunnery Mills, dating from 1796. One of the buildings has been demolished and replaced, while the other has been converted to riverside apartments. Records indicate that there was a mill on this site as early as 1643, providing flour and other products for the town of Douglas.

We shall walk the short distance into Douglas alongside the river from which the town's name is derived. Two rivers merge at Pulrose near the power station. The river Dhoo drains the central valley

and the river Glass drains the Baldwin valleys, and the two combine to form the Douglas river. As we walk over the bridge and look back along Leigh Terrace we can appreciate the style of the houses which were once the homes of the gentry of the town before it developed inland. We continue along the North Quay, passing the Steam Railway station and, as we walk to the bus station, observe the grey stone building with its gable end facing the harbour just before St Matthew's church. Look at the plaque in the wall which marks the site of the original Douglas Corporation power station. ❑

The Millennium Way

A 22-mile (35km) challenge. A very full day's walk of varied going. Refreshment available at Crosby, where an overnight stop is also possible. Advisable to take food on the walk

THE Millennium Way was opened at Easter, 1979, and it was adequately marked with the distinctive symbol, *below*. What was not foreseen was the fact that many would be collected by souvenir hunters. The Way remains, however, well marked on the rights of way map, and reasonably well marked on the ground.

It starts at the foot of Skyhill, near Ramsey, and directions on getting there by public transport are on *page 88*. At the outset, it was conceived that the route to Castletown could be walked in two halves with the break at Crosby.

The first part of the way is described in *Stage 3 of the Manx Meander, page 88* When we reach the mountain wall at the top of Sky Hill, we carry straight on over the open moorland on a rutted track (generally following a bearing of 198°) until we come to a very boggy area. The old *Via Regia*, as described in the *Chronicles of Mann*, veers to the left and follows the line of the present mountain road for some distance. To avoid walking on the busy road, the Millennium Way strikes off to the right, heading for the saddle between Slieau Managh (mountain of the monks) and Snaefell (snow mountain). There is a cairn on the skyline and we head for it, after carefully picking our way through the bog on the planks provided. The view to the left is of the North Barrule ridge, while on our right is the rounded top of Slieau Managh.

If the mist comes down, the mountain can be a very different place, compared with on a clear day and, although the Way is marked with concrete waymarkers, a compass is a desirable extra. The compass bearing is 220° which will take us past the cairn over the saddle, to join the mountain wall above Block Eary.

The bulk of Snaefell is ahead of us and the Way takes us over the western shoulder of the mountain. We follow the wall downhill. Looking to the right, we can see the reservoir and just make out the Sulby slate quarries. Beyond, we can see the Sulby Valley with Killabregga and Mount Karrin. We join a gully where the wall turns right and continue down that to cross the river at the bottom by the stile provided.

The Way now now strikes off steeply from the river and at right angles to it. It can be wet here at all times of the year, but only for a short distance. As we climb, it is worth looking back where we have just walked to see a number of round mounds which are the "shielings", where people lived with their animals on the mountain pasture during the summer months — another

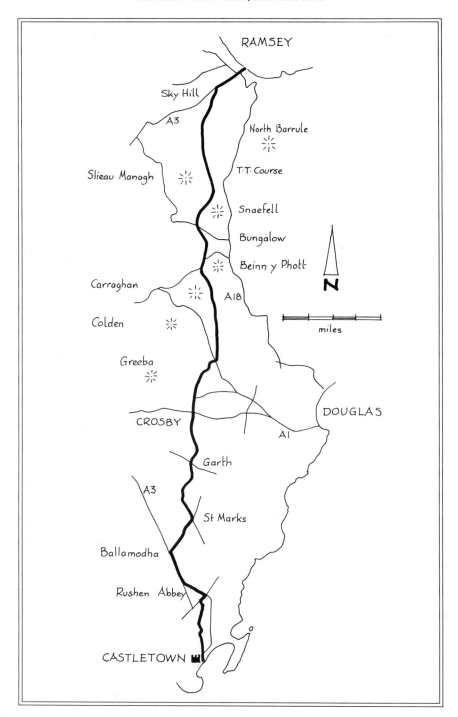

remnant of a past way of life and the best example of their kind on the island.

If you can pick up the line of the waymarkers, the going is easy. If not, follow a bearing of 226°. We should come across a stone wall and sod dyke which we follow to the Tholt y Will Road. The dyke is part of a very large ancient earthwork.

The Way strikes off across the valley of Beinn-y-Phott (very loosely interpreted as turf peak). At the bottom of the valley the river is crossed by an old stone bridge. We then climb the gully ahead of us on the left bank, passing the remains of yet another old mine working which was abandoned in 1867, having proved unproductive. At the head of the gully we have to be careful to follow the left fork on a bearing of 228°. If it is clear, we shall have no trouble seeing the signpost on the Brandywell Road.

Crossing the road, we are back on the line of the old Royal Way and we walk over the saddle between Beinn-y-Phott and Carraghyn, following a clear path until we meet a stone-surfaced road which we take to the left, and through the mountain gate. There is a view over the Baldwins and Douglas, with the south of the island and Langness visible in the distance.

We continue down into West Baldwin and, as we descend to St Luke's chapel of ease – which is well worth a stop to sign the visitors' book – we must look our for Cronk y Keeill Abban on the right where there is another ancient Tynwald site. At the bottom of the hill, we cross the bridge at West Baldwin and the way to Crosby is described in the *Manx Meander, page 92*.

Crosby is the point at which you can break the walk into two separate day walks. However, we shall press on down Station Road and up School Hill ahead of us, passing the old school. Our route stays on the surfaced road to Garth crossroads.

This was formerly a parochial church school and was built in 1874. It was typical of the type of school which provided the only education a child would get up to school-leaving age. In 1924, the school came under the control of the then newly formed Education Authority. The ostensibly remote location actually puts the school almost at the centre of the parish of Marown which it served and adjacent to our next stop, which is the old parish church at the top of the hill.

The original small church ascribed to St Runius can be directly traced to the 12th century, although there is a record of a keeill and Christian worship on this site since the 7th century. The church is worth a visit and is usually open. A potted history is available in return for a donation towards the upkeep of the fabric.

On the way up the hill to the Garth, we pass the site of St Patrick's Chair, a small group of stones which folklore tells us stand where St Patrick preached to the nation and blessed the Kingdom of Mann.

We go straight on at the cross roads, passing Ballanicholas and Campbell's Bridge, where we must stop and look at the interesting inscription on the plaque which shows that Douglas, Peel and Castletown are equidistant. The spoil heaps nearby locate the site of yet another mine which was opened as a trial but did not prove productive, although there is much zinc ore in the spoil. The bridge spans the Santon Burn which forms the boundary between the parish of Marown and Malew.

We continue to St Mark's, where the church provides a good landmark for us on the skyline ahead. The church was built at the instigation of Bishop Hildesley in the 18th century. The houses beside it were built to provide an income to support the adjoining school, now only used for church and village activities.

Be careful at the Old Parsonage – we have to turn right, following the waymarkers alongside the parsonage, and down the land crossing the meadow at the bottom at an angle, to cross the Awin Ruy (red river) by a stone slab. Just to our right, we can make a detour to an ancient monument which is described as Godred Crovan's stone and is part of the earthworks attached to the fort at Ballanicholas. Precisely what the connection is with the man who was the first King of Mann is not too clear. We return to the Millennium Way and follow the route through Ballamodha farm to the main road, where we turn left and walk down the road to the Athol Bridge at the bottom of Silverdale Hill. At the bridge, we turn left through Silverdale and Ballasalla and along the Silverburn, well described in *Walk 6, page 65*.

The Millennium Way, however, finishes at Castle Rushen in Castletown. From Rushen Abbey we follow the west wall, cross the main road, follow the waymarkers and join the Silverburn by some ruined buildings. The area is usually muddy as it is used as a shelter by cattle. The building was originally a cotton mill.

Walking down the river we may be lucky to see a train in full steam on the line which runs on a wall forming the opposite bank of the river. The Way crosses the river on a wooden bridge and we continue towards Castletown, passing Pulsom Park. On the opposite side of the river we can see the weir which took water for the impressive Golden Meadow Mill, which can be visited on certain open days. The building dates from the 15th century, although the machinery presently there dates from 1840 and it has recently been restored to working order.

We pass under the railway, emerging at Alexander Bridge to cross the road and walk along the harbour to the Castle. Return to Douglas from Castletown Station. ❏

The Coastal Footpath

RAAD NY FOILLAN

A 90-MILE (145km) walk. Can be walked in five strenuous days, with accommodation at convenient places. Setting out from Peel, the suggested staging points are Port St Mary, Douglas, and Ramsey. All are well served by public transport for those preferring to use Douglas as a base

MUCH of the spectacular Raad ny Foillan coincides quite closely with the route of the *Manx Meander*. As other sections closely follow the coastline, there are no detailed route maps provided. Refer to the map on *page 78* for the general route.

It is advisable to take food on each day's walk, as well as adequate clothing.

From Peel — where the path was formally opened in 1986 — we follow the *Manx Meander (stage 6)* as far as Glen Maye.

As we reach the mouth of the glen we take the path down the cliff to the footbridge over the river almost on the shore line, from where we follow the coastal footpath signs (a blue background with a white silhouette of a gull) and the waymarkers through some fields to the coast road which we continue along to Dalby village. Continuing through the village we must be careful to take a right fork along the Lag road (lag meaning hollow). The path crosses a stream on some stepping stones and there are always ducks present. The road deteriorates rapidly. We must be careful to take the right way up the hill between the hedges on the road known locally as "the slabs" for very obvious reasons.

At the top of this rocky area, the terrain opens out and we come to the boundary marker for the National Trust

land. It is here that we turn right, following the waymarkers once more and on a defined track. If you thought the view was good walking down the Lag, then the next mile holds some of the best views in the island — of sea and cliffs — and I never tire of them. The path is on a cliff edge here but quite safe. Be careful to cross the boundary wall by the stile provided, otherwise you may find yourself walking down a zigzag path to Feustal and it is a long way back up. So we maintain our height and walk along the cliff top to Gob ny Ushtey, crossing the stream at Glion Mooar, to walk up across the moorland towards the white house in the distance. This is a venture centre situated in the old farm buildings of Eary Cushlin but our path is to the right of it and strikes up the slope of Cronk ny Irree Laa to rejoin *Stage 6* of the *Manx Meander* on the summit. It is worth a pause to admire the view all round and to consider the exposed position of the hill fort in which we stand.

The next section of the path from the top of Cronk ny Irree Laa as far as Santon Head, beyond Castletown, coincides with that of the *Manx Meander*, with the exception of a slight variation at the Sloc beside the sheep pens and picnic tables. From here we climb to the top of Lhiat-

Above: The bay at Niarbyl, a worthwhile detour from the coastal path at Dalby, from where the view — left — extends to the southern tip of the island

tee ny Biennee, which, in the other route, is skirted to the east. The route is way-marked, but not very clearly (the bearing is 275°), and the climb is not for the faint-hearted. But the views back towards Peel and Niarbyl are worth the effort. The path from here is indistinct but mainly follows the cairns along the broad ridge of the Carnanes.

It is possible to walk along the edge of the cliff but not advisable if the mist comes in off the sea. If that happens, take a bearing of 205° and you will come out on the lower path above Fleshwick. If you have no head for heights, you would be well advised to stick to the lower path followed by the *Manx*

Meander. From Santon Head, the Raad ny Foillan deviates slightly from the *Meander*, sticking to the coast a little further to Balnahowe. Before turning inland, the view north of Pistol Castle and Little Ness is worth savouring. The path heads inland to rejoin the other route again for a short distance from Ballaquiggin railway bridge, past Crogga, but turns right at Ballaveare (map reference 342734) to join *Walk 5, page 61*, at Port Soderick railway station, then on to Douglas.

The Coastal Path continues along the promenade past the horse tram depot and electric tram depot, following the coast and Seaview Road, where some spectacularly placed houses have been built on the site of the former White City amusement park. No longer is there the sound of the old National gas engine thumping away to send the cars rumbling and clattering around the figure of eight — happy memories!

Back on the main road, we walk a short distance round the head of Onchan Harbour. We then have to take care to follow the waymarkers down a grass track which was part of the original layout of the Douglas Bay Estate, linked with the development of the electric tramway. It soon degenerates into a path which threads it way through what appear to be the front gardens of some very well appointed houses. Don't be deterred — the path was there first and I can clearly remember clambering up this headland when it was just fields to look at the wreck of the trawler *Mary Healey*.

We soon rejoin the coast road and walk alongside the tramway until we reach Groudle, turning right, down the Old Groudle beach road, then crossing the footbridge at the bottom and climbing the path to cross the Groudle Railway. From here, we go straight on to join a surfaced roadway which we follow for approximately a mile, before turning right over farmland at Ballacreggan to Clayhead. Before that it is worth making a short detour to Lonan Old Parish Church (map reference 426796), where the particular thing to look for is the tenth century Celtic wheel-headed cross slab.

As we join the Clay Head road, the view north over Laxey Bay opens up as far as Maughold Head. We make our way almost to Baldrine, turning right along the fisherman's path to Garwick Beach. Cross the stream and leave the shore beside the boathouse to walk back uphill to the Coast Road where we find ourselves beside the tram track again. Garwick was one of the island's Victorian watering places, with a hotel, glen and rowing boats on the beach. Our pace of life these days does not seem to allow such simple pleasures, which is a great shame.

We have to walk along the road here for a while and it can be a bit tiresome, with no pavement and traffic flashing by. We shall soon leave it behind as we head off past Fairy Cottage down Old Laxey Hill towards the shore. If the tide is right — check the time of low water — you can take an interesting alternative route from Fairy Cottage to Laxey harbour. You must follow the sign which warns you that the path is tidal over the headland and down to the shore at Goby-Rheym. The view of Laxey beach is worth the effort, even if the tide is in and you have to go back to Fairy Cottage again.

Half way down Old Laxey Hill, after crossing the tram track, we drop on to the promenade by way of the steps in the cliff. In the summer you can have a choice of places to stop for a break. In winter, if you have not brought food with you, you may have to go up into the village to eat. The harbour at Laxey is always a pleasant spot and we walk round the head of the harbour and over the bridge to take the old packhorse road straight up the hill. We cross the tram track and the coast road to carry on uphill to join the Ballaragh road.

It is worth stopping for a breather to look back over Laxey. We carry on over Ballaragh and, as we pass the old chapel, we can see up towards Snaefell and the mines, which are easily identified by the spoil heaps.

At the top of the hill, as we turn the corner, we must be careful not to miss the path on the apex of the bend which we follow across the road and the tram track to the Dhoon loop road, where we can explore the tram depot and the sidings described in the tram ride to start *Walk 3, page 57.*

I am going to suggest you take an energetic alternative here to test your stamina. As we join the loop road from

Ballaragh, just hop over the stile and then back to the adjacent green lane, which is the old road to Dhoon beach. As we zig-zag down to the sea, we can see the Dhoon slate cliffs sloping steeply. The beach is very stony but it is worth spending a little while exploring the unusual rock formations, tide permitting, before making our way back to the road. The climb up the glen is strenuous, but worth the effort.

Soon we come to the pool at the bottom of the two falls which together form the biggest waterfall in the island. The path, on its way up, affords us differing views of the Dhoon falls. The glen covers 44 acres and offers the naturalist myriad species of trees and woodland flora. As we level out in the upper part of the glen we come across yet another mining relic. The large wheelcase housed the 50ft diameter wheel of the Dhoon mine, belonging to the Rhennie Laxey Mining Company. Although worked for ten years or so, it was never productive, being one of the lesser trials to find extensions of the Laxey vein.

We are soon back at the road, having taken more than an hour to make about 50 yards progress along the loop road, thanks to my diversion. The next two miles (4km) are on surfaced roads, but they are narrow and rural, so we can put up with it as we follow the waymarkers to the ford at Glen Mona. We have to bear right before the ford and follow the public road down the side of the lower Cornah valley to Port Cornah, being careful at the Barony entrance to veer left and keep going downhill.

Port Cornah is a tidal saltmarsh and a good place to view waders. We walk across the saltmarsh on the path and cross the Cornah river by the footbridge to walk up Benussi's Lane, through the woodland of the Cornah valley. We cross the tram track and the coast road again, to continue up the Beyr ny Quarkeryn (the Quakers' Road).

At the top of the hill we shall come across the Quakers' burial ground where William Callow and other persecuted Quakers lie buried in now peaceful surroundings. Shortly after leaving this sanctuary we descend into Ballajora, with Maughold Head providing the backdrop to the way ahead.

At Ballajora tram stop we join the route described in *Walk 4, page 59*, as far as Port-e-Vullen, where we take the Coastal Path, if the tide permits, round the headland of Gob-ny-Rona, to rejoin the road which we follow uphill over the tram track at Belle Vue halt, to the coast road.

We turn right and follow the road down to Ballure Glen and walk down the glen to the shore. As we walk into the glen we can see on our left the twin span of the Ballure bridge carrying the tramway, each span being 237ft (73m). It was built in 1899. Interestingly enough, the area on our right, by the tram track, was the terminus for Ramsey in 1898 and it was to be another year before it reached its present stop in the town itself.

If the tide is in our favour, we can walk into Ramsey along the foreshore under the Queen's Pier, and on to the promenade by the lifeboat house. From Ramsey, cross the harbour on the town bridge and head north along the promenade, and on to the shore walking to the Point of Ayre under Shellag Point, where the sand cliffs are constantly being eroded. If the wind is onshore and it is one hour either side of high water, then we must take the road to Cranstal as the shoreline becomes impassable.

As we walked along the shore, did you notice some cast iron pipes lying haphazard and broken from time to time? Don't be alarmed, it was not a broken sewage outfall, but simply the remains of the pipeline which conveyed brine from a borehole at the Point of Ayre — where it was extracted by a

The wheelcase of the Dhoon Rhennie Mine in the beautiful Dhoon Glen

steam driven pump — to the salt works at Ramsey. The whole operation was run by the Manx Salt and Alkali Company and the product was used locally and exported using the company's own steam coaster. The works closed in the 1950s but some remnants of the pump house and reservoir can be still seen at the Point of Ayre.

The Point of Ayre lighthouse is worth more than a passing glance. It was designed by Robert Stevenson (grandfather of Robert Louis) and completed in 1818. It is open to the public at certain times.

The Coastal Path continues round the Point and along the north-west coast of the island, between the dunes and the sea. The going is heavy underfoot but the reward comes from the wealth of

117

bird life. By far the most graceful for me is the gannet which can be seen in late summer and autumn in great numbers. Call at the Ayre's Visitor Centre on National Trust land, to find out more about the natural history.

The words of the Manx poet TE Brown, learnt at school by many of the island's children, spring to mind, here.

BELLA GORY
Westward to Jurby, eastward if you look,
The coast runs level to the Point of Ayre,
A waste of land, sea holly, and wild
thyme —
Wild thyme and bent. The Mull of Gallo-
way
Is opposite. Adown the farthest west,
Not visible now, lie stretched the hills of
Mourne.

As we round Jurby Head, the sand cliffs become higher and the beach more stony. If we are passing at low water, we may see the remains of the Fleetwood trawler, *Passages,* which was driven ashore in 1929 by a north-westerly gale when returning from the Icelandic fishing grounds. The shoreline from here to Orrisdale Head is the habitat for large flocks of oystercatchers and curlews. It is also an area of coast subject to extensive erosion by the sea and we can see large sections of concrete walkway from wartime lookouts, hanging over the cliff edge. The area is still used as an observation post in connection with a Nato bombing range just off the coast. Near Ballaugh Cronk is the site of a radar installation, recently removed, which was associated with the range.

As we draw level with Orrisdale Head, we must keep a good look out for the sign directing us off the shore at Glen Trunk (map reference 317923). We follow the Coastal Path waymarkers to join the disused railway track at Rhencullen, turning right to follow it to Kirk Michael where it gives a good approach to the parish church. We come into the old railway station and observe a novel use for the old buildings. These are now the Kirk Michael fire station, housing two modern appliances for the retained brigade which covers a large area of the west of the island.

We cross the road and continue on the railway track a short distance to Glen Wyllin, zig-zagging down into the glen under the masonry piers which used to carry the Ramsey line over the glen on three spans. The Isle of Man Railway Company purchased the glen in 1935 and it was developed as a pleasure ground with bowling greens, swings, roundabouts, a boating lake and a café. It was a mecca for Sunday School picnics after the war. Now used as a camp site, the signs of its former glory can be seen here and there.

We join the shore once more and walk only as far as Glen Mooar, a distance of about half a mile. You can see for yourself the extent of the erosion at this area and, in 1982, there was a severe storm, coupled with heavy rain, which caused large sections of the adjoining sand cliff to collapse.

We walk up the Glen Mooar beach road to join and cross the coast road, following the signpost into the upper part of the glen. Ahead of us are the remains of the Glen Mooar railway viaduct. We climb up the side of the abutment of the viaduct to join the railway track again, which we follow for about three miles (5km) to St German's halt.

The section above Gob-y-Deigan, which has always been subject to subsidence, illustrates vividly how exposed this section of the railway was to the elements. A turntable was installed at St John's to enable carriages to be turned so that they weathered evenly *(see also page 26).* At the halt, we join the coast road again, turning right shortly to join the route described in the *Manx Meander, Stage 5,* as we walk along the headland to Peel. ❏

The Herring Way

A 14-mile (23km) walk with good eating facilities at several points along the way. Takes in industrial archaeological sites and other places of historic interest touched on in some of the other walks

THE Bayr ny Skeddan is, as the name implies, based on an ancient herring road and, as with all the long distance paths in the island, a few liberties have been taken along the way.

Like the coastal walk, this path was also introduced in Heritage Year and it too starts at the old water tank at the former railway station at Peel. It takes the same route as the *Coastal Path* as far as Glen Maye. At Glen Maye, as we round the headland, we walk up the glen, as described in the *Manx Meander, Stage 6*, and join the main road to walk right to the bottom of the hill and left along the Sound Road.

Here we leave the *Manx Meander* and must take care, in the old part of Glen Maye, to turn left after a short distance to follow the public right of way down to the river, which we cross on the postman's path, and climb up the opposite side of the river to join the Glen Rushen road. This is now closed to traffic because of a landslip, which we cross with care and continue up the valley on the old road. If we look across the river and up on the side of Dalby mountain, we can see

BAYR NY SKEDDAN

HERITAGE YEAR 1986

THE KING OF THE SEA

Up with the lug and let her run before the wind and tide

The gannets plunge, the gulls keep watch the herring shoal is wide

Oh! the herring, boys, the herring, Oh! the herring, boys, for me!

Red or kipper'd, fresh or pickled, Oh! the herring is the king of the sea!

Song by JF Gill, published in 1896

clearly the levels of the Glen Rushen Slate Quarries which were described earlier. Pause and consider the exposed conditions in which the 120 quarrymen had to work.

After a short distance, we emerge from the tree cover and take a right fork, passing some ruined cottages on the left, connected with the Glen Rushen mines which are now on the hill above us and on our left as we continue up the valley alongside the Glen Rushen river. We arrive eventually at a water supply intake at the end of the road.

Here we follow the waymarkers over the gate on the right and walk up the hillside below the plantation at the Lhargan. The path crosses the fence into the plantation a little way up the hill and this is the place to stop and look back down the valley. Ahead of us on the opposite hill are the surface remains of Beckwith's Mine, with its crooked chimney and engine house. In the distance, on the skyline, is the engine house and chimney at Snuff the Wind which was Cross's Mine. Both mines are described in the *Industrial Heritage section* at the start of the book.

The path is clearly followed over a plantation road on Dalby Mountain and we eventually reach the main road, which we follow to the left for about a mile to the Round Table crossroads.

Straight ahead of us is South Barrule (the word Barrule is derived from the Scandinavian word Vovoufjall meaning ward mountain — it was one of the hills used for watch and ward). On a clear day it is worth a short detour to the top to enjoy the magnificent views of the south of the island. On the way back down there are good views over Cronk Fedjag and Cronk ny Irree Laa.

However, we must press straight on over the crossroads and, after a very short distance, take the track to the left. Now we really are on the old herring road leading to Castletown from Dalby and used by fishermen taking their catch overland for sale at the capital. When you consider their small craft and the fact that the herring were first caught in the seas off the west coast, this seemingly long trek was not so silly. Just consider the problems of beating your way in a small sailing craft, at the whim of the wind, round the south of the island. There was no harbour at Dalby, but the boats were hauled onto the grass above Traie Vane which was a good, safe landing place.

On our right we can glimpse now and again the Cringle Reservoir supplying water to the southern towns.

At the next crossroads, the Bayr ny Skeddan turns left and leaves the ancient route of the herring road. I suspect that this has been done to avoid the monotony of walking too far on surfaced roadways.

We follow the route markers along the Corlea Road and then to the right off

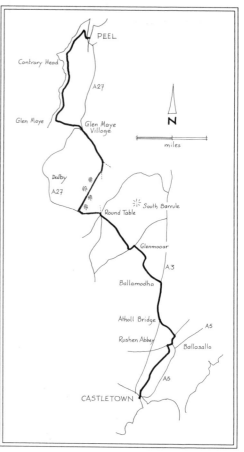

the road and down through Glion Cam (the winding glen), taking care not to lose our way at the farm at Glen Mooar. The going can be muddy at all times of the year, so we shall have to pick our way until the track becomes more distinct. We cross the Awin ny Reash (river of the moor) and join a surfaced track which we follow to the main road at the Ballamodha Straight, where we join the *Millennium Way to Castletown as described earlier.* ❑

The Heritage Trail

An 11-mile (18km) walk along the disused trackbed of the former steam railway from Douglas to Peel

STARTING at Douglas, we have to walk along the Peel Road to the Quarterbridge, where the trail starts.

The Peel line left Douglas station and ran parallel to the line to Port Erin, beside Hills Meadow industrial site, and we can clearly see the route it took to pass under the bridge where the Pulrose Road leads off towards the power station. After that, the track is obliterated by building development. The line crossed the River Glass behind the island's principal fire station on a skew lattice girder bridge, to emerge behind the Quarterbridge Hotel and cross the Castletown Road on a level crossing where the old gatehouse can still be seen.

The Heritage Trail starts here and follows the old railway parallel to the road. The trackbed is surfaced and now provides the only road link to land within the TT course when it is closed for motorcycle racing. On our left we have a good view of Kirby Park, a haunt of the heron (in Manx, *Coar ny Hastan*). The way then passes under the Peel road at Braddan and the parish church can be seen to our left beyond the river.

The surfaced road finishes and we soon come onto the old railway bed and follow the river Dhoo to Union Mills which was the site of the first station. There was a halt at Braddan which was used in connection with open-air church services on summer Sunday mornings.

As part of this heritage project, the Adult Training Centre has refurbished a number of lineside buildings in conjunction with the government department responsible for rights of way. Lineside descriptions and picnic areas have been provided along the length of the walk.

At Union Mills, we have to leave the track and cross the main road, rejoining the railway behind the Union Mills industrial estate. The Union Mills were so named because two mills were situated on the site, one for wool and one for corn, and both drew water from the same dam. The outline of the mill buildings is still clearly seen.

THE HERITAGE TRAIL

Leaving the mills, we soon enter the central valley and its wild beauty remains unchanged from when the railway was built, except for the overhead power lines which we soon come across as we approach the level crossing at Close Mooar.

The next section of the way leads to Crosby, with a good view of Greeba ahead of us and Creg-y-Whallian to the left, indicating the gap through which the railway went on its way to Peel. We pass the new parish church of Marown before coming to Crosby station.

The section between Crosby and Bal-

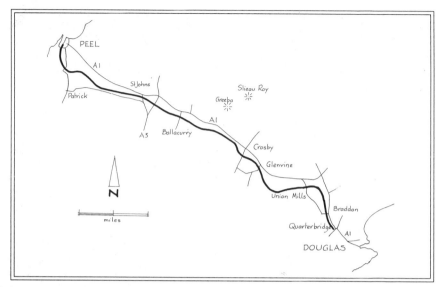

lacurry is described in *Walk 9, page 72.* Just before Ballacurry level crossing, we reach the highest point on the railway at 183ft (56.3 metres) above sea level. From now on it is all downhill.

The next section of railway track has been used previously as a training run for racehorses from a nearby stud, but we are now likely to be the only people using this area. We leave the Curragh area of the central valley and cross the main road to Castletown at the Curragh Road crossing, with its gatehouse, entering St John's under the shadow of Slieau Whallian. The sandpits — on the left before passing under the bridge which took the Foxdale branch line — were used by the railway company for sand extraction and numerous temporary sidings were built to service them. Passing under the bridge, the open area ahead is the site of St John's station. There were once three stations here, but now the only tangible signs are the remains of the signal box and a cattle dock.

We cross the Station Road and walk smartly past the sewage works to regain the railway. We can see the broad permanent way ahead of us. This was where the Peel and Ramsey lines ran parallel out of St John's. The trains always left together and it always appeared as if they were racing. The Ramsey train would work hard to take a run at the bank which climbed at a gradient of 1 in 132, swinging away to the right over the Douglas to Peel road, while the Peel train accelerated away to the left down a gradient of 1 in 80.

We cross the River Neb over the railway bridge and continue downhill all the way on easier gradients, passing Shenharra and the site of the Abbey brickworks. Ahead of us is Corrin's Hill, with its folly, and Peel Hill to the right. We pass through a cutting to swing round below Peel golf course among willow and *curragh* near the river.

As we swing right towards Peel and close to the river, keep a sharp look out for signs of the old abutments for the Knockaloe branch line where it crossed the river on a sharp curve to head up across the fields, parallel to the road, before crossing it to gain access to Knockaloe itself. The branch was built in 1915 to serve an internment camp for

*Above: A nostalgic view of MER locomotive No.11, Maitland, at Union Mills. **Below:** The Ramsey line climbed away on a gradient of 1 in 132 from St John's, hence the double-heading in this view*

"aliens" during the first world war. On cessation of hostilities, the track was removed and very little trace remains.

As we approach the last half-mile into Peel, we pass under the Glenfaba road bridge alongside the Glenfaba Mill, now a private residence. Much of the original structure, dating from 1850, survives, and the wheel can be seen alongside the railway.

We enter Peel "through the back door", passing the power station and the Mill Road industrial estate to finish at the old water tower of Peel Station.
See Peel City Trail, page 42. ❏

by tram

by train

by foot

BY SEA

When travelling is as important to you as your destination,
make sure that you take the ferry.
Because arriving by sea is the perfect way to appreciate the
beauty of our island right from the start.
The horse trams and buses start right on the pier, and the
steam trains are just a stone's throw away.
If you like to have your car to meander around our island at
your own pace, this can come on the ferry too!
For further information contact the Isle of Man Steam Packet
Company on Douglas 0624 661661.
We also can provide you with all you need for a short
break – just ask for our Magic Holiday brochure.

Useful information

Museums

The Manx Museum, Crellin's Hill, Douglas. Headquarters of the national museum service and the Manx National Trust, with extensive collections ranging from prehistory to the present day. Building also houses the National Art Gallery and the National Reference Library. ☎ 675522

MANX MUSEUM OUTSTATIONS —

Grove Museum of Rural Life, Ramsey. Fine Victorian residence with period displays. Buses 20A and 20B from Ramsey.

Nautical Museum, Castletown. Main feature is the 18th century armed yacht, Peggy. Steam railway or buses 1, 1A and 8 to Castletown.

Cregneash Village Folk Museum. Housed in traditional restored Manx cottages. Bus 1A (*see Walk 8*).

Murrays Motorcycle Museum. A must for TT fans. Bungalow station, Snaefell Railway. ☎ 781719

Crosby Motor Museum. Remarkable collection of vintage vehicles, visited on the *Manx Meander*. Bus 5 or 6. ☎ 851236

Laxey Heritage Trust (for information on the Mines Trail). Manx Electric Railway to Laxey. ☎ 862007

Odin's Raven. Replica Viking long boat, Peel harbour. ☎ 843300

RAILWAY MUSEUMS —

Steam railway, Port Erin station. Electric railway, Ramsey station. Trams, Douglas Corporation terminus, Derby Castle. Department of Transport, ☎ 663366.

Wildlife and animals

NATIONAL GLENS

Some of the finest scenery in the Isle of Man is to be found in the lush glens where the rivers which rise in the central highlands have carved deep valleys on their way to the sea.

The waterfall in picturesque Dhoon Glen

The glens are many, but to be particularly recommended are: Dhoon Glen, on the Manx Electric Railway; Groudle Glen, visited on *Walk 1*; Glen Maye, bus 7 (also visited on the *Manx Meander*); Sulby Glen, bus 5 or 6, or walk down the glen from Bungalow Station on the Snaefell railway.

Curraghs Wildlife Park, Ballaugh, bus 5 or 6. ☎ 897323

Home of Rest for Old Horses (retired from the Douglas trams), Bulrhenny, Richmond Hill, Douglas. ☎ 674594

Aquarium, Liverpool University Marine Biological Station, Port Erin harbour. Steam train, or buses 1, 1A or 8 to Port Erin.

Tynwald National Park. Arboretum at St John's. Buses 5 and 6.

Bird watching and nature trails — Ayres visitor centre, Buses 20A and 20B to Point of Ayre; boat trips to the Calf of Man, Port Erin harbour — see end of breakwater for sailing times.

Transport and information

Railways, Strathallan Crescent, Douglas
☎ 663366
Bus station, Lord Street, Douglas ☎ 662525
Department of Tourism, Victoria Street, Douglas ☎ 686766
Isle of Man Steam Packet Seaways ☎ 661661

Traditional Manx Loaghtan sheep can be seen at Cregneash museum, and on the Calf of Man

The Manx cat — pure bred tailless cats are scarce since the closure of the Manx Cattery in Douglas

Manx Airlines ☎ 824313
Cycle hire — Castletown Cycles ☎ 823587; Callow Cycles, Douglas ☎ 675340, Jayne White Cycles, Douglas ☎ 624909; Ramsey Cycles ☎ 814076, Pedal Power, Douglas ☎ 662026.
Horse riding — Tromode Farm Stables, Douglas ☎ 676717

Bibliography and recommended reading

General

Portrait of the Isle of Man, EH Stenning

The Isle of Man, RH Kinvig, *Liverpool University Press*

The Place Names of the Isle of Man, JJ Kneen

100 Years of Heritage, *Manx Museum*

Geology of the Isle of Man, GW Lamplugh

The Story of the Isle of Man, CW Airne

Prehistoric Sites in the Isle of Man, *Manx Museum*

Industrial Archaeology of the Isle of Man, Bawden, Garrad, Qualtrough, Scatchard

Peel, Fred Palmer

A History of Manx Gardens, Garrad, *Collector's Choice*

The Ancient and Historic Monuments of the Isle of Man, *Manx Museum*

Isle of Man Coastal Footpath, Aileen Evans, *Cicerone Press*

Transport

Isle of Man Tramways, FK Pearson, *David & Charles*

The Isle of Man Railway, JIC Boyd, *Oakwood*

The Manx Transport Systems, W Lambden, *The Omnibus Society*

A Guide to the Steam Railways of Great Britain, Ed W Awdry and Chris Cooke, *Pelham Books*

Narrow Gauge Railways of the British Isles, PB Whitehouse and JB Snell, *Book Club Associates*

Isle of Man Railway, and Manx Electric Railway, both by Hendry & Hendry (*published by Isle of Man Railways*)

Groudle Glen Railway, *published by the Groudle Glen Railway Ltd*

Books on the Isle of Man from Leading Edge

Mann Ablaze! — *A History of the Isle of Man Fire Service*
By the author of the Isle of Man by Tram, Train and Foot, Stan Basnett's account is a valuable social document, as well as a must for transport and fire-fighting enthusiasts.
ISBN 0 948135 25 5. £6.75

With Heart, Soul and Voice — *100 years of the Manx Music Festival*
Martin Faragher tells the fascinating story of how a national music festival became an integral part of Manx way of life. A book that will appeal to anyone interested in music or Celtic culture.
ISBN 0 948135 32 8. £5.95

Forthcoming titles

100 Years of the Manx Electric Railway
To mark the centenary of the MER, Leading Edge is publishing in autumn 1992 this new edition of Frank Pearson's comprehensive work, Isle of Man Tramways, first published in 1970. The new edition concentrates on the MER and the Snaefell Mountain Railway and contains much new material and photographs.
ISBN 0 948135 38 7. Price to be advised.

Hidden Places of Mann
Stan Basnett's sequel to the Isle of Man by Tram,Train and Foot takes the reader off the beaten track to unveil some little visited corners and reveal new insights into the Island's fascinating past. Once again, the book is aimed primarily at users of the extensive Manx rail and bus network. Due for publication spring 1993.
ISBN 0 948135 39 5. Price to be advised.

See our sales address, over.